THE TICKLE BOX TALES

by Marlene Russell Lovejoy

DORRANCE
PUBLISHING CO
EST. 1920
PITTSBURGH, PENNSYLVANIA 15238

Dorrance Publishing Co
585 Alpha Drive
Pittsburgh, PA 15238
Visit our website at *www.dorrancebookstore.com*

ISBN: 978-1-6480-4507-3
eISBN: 978-1-6480-4484-7

THE TICKLE
BOX TALES

A merry heart
doeth good like a medicine.

- Proverbs 17:22 from the Bible

Introduction

When we were young and giggly, Kathi's Dad said, "You girls have turned over your tickle boxes." As a kid, I was intrigued with the phrase "tickle box," and I still am.

In the following true stories, smile, and unlock your place of laughter. Recapture the childlike you, and find your sunny spot. Some stories will remind you of events or people from your past. Good. You will feel at home. You will encounter other characters in my family and friends whose stories were too scrumptious to leave on the floor among the endless stacks of papers. These recollections, essays, and stories are one way to explain my phenomenology, or the world as I experienced it. My memories are the impressions and scenes from my mind's eye that were stored deep within the recesses of my brain.

I have spent hours, days, and years extrapolating moments from my past, only to discover my siblings have different recollections of our shared youth. Our minds retain bits and pieces of an event, a version unique to each of us. We recall an event, and later discover we "mis-remembered" what occurred. How does that happen? Good question. Our minds are complex entities. Possibly, my discombobulated recollections stemmed from significant blows to my head during childhood. Oh, no, hold that thought. That story line is later on. Back to this epistle. From an early age, I jotted down notes, catchy phrases, verses, sayings, and stories on napkins, scraps of paper, and church bulletins. I loved words, so I stashed away these wonderful nuggets of gold that I admired. My compilation stitched together shows a microcosm of me: my little world of what I did, how I thought, and who I encountered. My voice shows authenticity, and my honesty is obvious. Plus, I expound on particular time periods to give the stories their place in history. Some pieces are only there as pure entertainment.

In spite of my writing skills, or lack thereof, my book is a gift for my family and friends. I want them to enjoy and know these stories. As I have written, I have spent time alone with God, praying for the best words to convey my thoughts. Whenever I write, I have verbal fights with the words. I toss them around and seek better words until I can pin down the best one. In the final "knockdown, drag out" with words, carefully I extract the specific verbiage that makes the final cut. As the reader, you may sense something: I have fun writing stories and essays. Maybe you will get caught in the breeze of lightheartedness and experience a snippet of joy yourself.

Many details from the past are lost or hidden; some of our particular ancestors did not leave many traces of their daily lives. No time or energy was left at the end of their weary days to jot down any details. If I could step back in time, it would be delightful to see events such as my mother and her family's trip to New York City in 1939 to see the World's Fair. Or see the grand opening of *Gone with the Wind* in Atlanta with the Hollywood stars in attendance.

Table of Contents

Chapter 1

WAY BACK YONDER

1. OUR PEOPLE

We were the Russells, Elliotts, and Knights who were teachers, preachers, and farmers, like many Southerners in the 1800s. Our ministers started churches around Georgia that are still open today. The Russell sisters taught hundreds of students, and then their children and grandchildren.

Our great grandmother, Mollie (Mary Watts) Elliott was born in Rockdale County in 1865, at the end of the Civil War (or War Between the States). When she was six weeks old, her family moved to Henry County.

In 1884, at the age of 19, Mollie was whisked away in a horse and buggy to marry Joel Jefferson Knight. Before they left, her brother Roll (Raleigh) ran out to offer a deal:

"Mr. Knight, I will give you my goat and wagon, if you won't take my sis Mollie away."

J.J. refused the tempting offer and away they trotted. As a young bride, she recalled the hard life: "I drew my own water from a well, boiled clothes in an old washpot, and beat them on a batting bench (washboard). We had to raise everything we ate, except coffee and sugar. We only used sugar in our coffee on Sunday mornings[1].

"We lived in a little log cabin, and only half of its windows were glass. We had it sorta hard, but people loved each other better, and had more time to visit."

Jefferson and Mollie Knight had 11 children and gave us a part of our amazing heritage and family lineage.

We knew her as Granny Knight, and she lived through many events—numerous wars, the invention of the radio, car, television, planes, computers, and satellites—more changes than anyone can imagine during her 103 years.

Before she died in 1968, she still sat in front of the mirror every morning and fixed her hair. She ate breakfast and quietly read the <u>Bible</u> which had sustained her throughout her life. What a devout believer!

2. OUR RUSSELL GRANDPARENTS

One of their daughters, Martha Cleo, married Grover B. Russell. They were our grandparents, Granddaddy and Grandmother Russell. With the help of their seven children, they farmed and eked out a living.

Granddaddy was a tough, hardworking man, and no one dared to cross him. We never even talked or laughed at the dinner table. As the farming life became difficult, Grandaddy decided to move to the little town of McDonough five miles away. Their house was on a main street and only a few blocks to the town square, the Presbyterian Church where they attended; and to Planters' Warehouse, where Granddaddy got a job. They walked many places, but did have a car for an occasional drive to the country, or to college to visit their daughters.

Granddaddy was a smart man. When given the exact measurements of a house, he could calculate how many bricks it would take to build it, within three to four bricks. Our daddy as a boy watched him standing in the front yard, talking to a neighbor who stopped by. Granddaddy took a piece of paper to mold his cigarette; he reached into his pocket for his Prince Albert tobacco, and tapped the leaves into the paper. He rolled the cigarette and licked the edges to seal it. As he lit up his cigarette or smoke, Daddy's little eyes took in every detail. Then, Daddy imitated him and made his own cigarette. He rolled up a little paper, dropped in some crushed leaves, and sealed it. Next, he pretended to smoke it, just like his Daddy.

3. NIGHTLY CREATURES

Sometimes, we spent the night with them in their old house. The "we" was my brother and sisters, but we did not all stay at the same time. Unbeknownst to us, their house hosted some attic creatures who liked to hang out. One night, several of these creepy things flew out and circled the ceiling. We had certainly never seen these creatures inside a house. Being totally cool, calm and collected kids, we screamed at the top of our lungs, "Bats! Bats!"

So, the bats flew faster around the rooms as if we were cheering them on. They seemed to like the attention. Our grandparents immediately armed themselves with brooms (their weapon of choice) and chased them as they zoomed toward the ceiling. They darted from one corner to another as we watched in horror. Then, the crazed critters zoomed into the hallway, performing a spectacular aerial show. Our grandparents were not amused. Granddaddy and Grandmother whacked at them and brought one down every now and then. They seemed to know what they were doing (our grandparents, as well as the bats).

Here is the thing about bats; they are nocturnal creatures. That means they sleep during the day and come out at night to scare the living daylights out of people. It works! Also, it is the time they feed. We prayed we did not look delicious.

Finally, the bats either left or were doomed by the brooms. I don't know exactly what happened; I was very busy screaming and running from here to there.

Two things I do know: we had never seen our grandparents move that quickly. And, we had never witnessed them having such a noisy and wild time in their entire lives. It was a doozy! If we had not been scared out of our wits, we probably would have enjoyed their escapades. When we finally settled down for bed, it was the first time I really understood the meaning of sleeping with one eye open.

4. A SURPRISE

Grandmother and Granddaddy Russell had the most wonderful screen porch and swing. We spent many hours reading in that swing, and more hours playing under their giant magnolia trees. Our cousins joined us in crushing the seeds to make Indian food or drawing in the dirt. Later, Grandmother used her brush broom to draw straight lines in the dirt to look nice. Then, Grandmother came out, "Cutting the watermelon 'ta-rectly' (directly)."

We ran to the back yard, where a beautiful, dark green watermelon, was resting on the picnic table, ready to be carved with her giant kitchen knife. She sliced us pieces containing the heart of the melon...the reddest and sweetest. Some of us sprinkled salt on it. We enjoyed the coldest and most delicious watermelon in the universe.

Then, she delighted us by taking the rind, the lightest green part, and carefully carving a row of teeth. She left big spaces between the teeth that lent a comical look. When she put the set into her mouth, and talked, her words slurred together, and out slid the rind. We did not understand a word she said. She got tickled, and we laughed until our sides hurt. She was hilarious; a side of her we had never seen. We begged for our own "set of teeth," to wear. She taught us how to slice our curved row of teeth. We tried them out, already laughing. The challenge was keeping the slippery rind teeth in as we talked. We jabbered a minute, and out they came! Gusts of laughter and fun.

That was the only funny thing we ever saw her do, but it was worth 100 things. We began our own family tradition of "rind teeth." I have never met but one person who has heard of the art of making rind teeth. You can bet your bottom dollar it was a Southerner.

5. WHAT TIRE?

Our grandparents only drove their car to church, to visit a relative, or occasionally to visit their children in college. Often, the roads were unpaved, so they endured dusty, dirt trails, or muddy, worn paths bumping over large tree roots and rocks. Gullies and big dips were left as soil was washed away by torrential rainstorms, often called "chicken or frog stranglers." My granddaddy was a stern, no non-sense kind of man who spoke very few words. If he smiled, it was purely accidental. My grandmother did not say or smile much, either. (If I was raising seven children, I would be speechless, too.)

One day as they were taking a Sunday drive and being tossed about as usual, Cleo said, "Grover, something is wrong."

"Naw, ain't nothing wrong, just a rough road," he said gruffly.

A minute later, "Grover, I think we lost a tire."

"Naw."

"Well, look…there goes one of our tires rolling and bouncing down yonder through that field."

I was surprised he didn't say, "Cleo, that's **NOT** our tire."

6. THREE MESSAGES FROM GOD

My husband's family grew up in Thomson, Georgia, and he visited there many times as he was growing up. His grandfather is connected with one of the following stories. One of the most devastating storms of McDuffie County (Thomson, GA) occurred on March 23, 1875. The most bizarre event happened at Henry Ivy's house; his horse was blown into the well. With the ingenuity of the men and their strength, they hoisted him out. Luckily, he was not seriously hurt and survived his first flight.

Eleven years later, an earthquake shook the county on August 31, 1886. Dishes were falling off the shelves, and out of the cupboards. Chimneys were tottering, and crashing to the ground. The most startling result of the quake came at a camp meeting being held at Fountain Campground. The earth was trembling as was the preacher who stood down front holding the revival service. Many sinners were converted in record time and unprecedented numbers. You can imagine people rushing down to the altar to be saved; all were thinking it was the end of the world.

After the dust settled, the hollering descended to lower decibels, and the congregation's hysteria quieted down considerably. Low murmurs and a steady hum were heard with endless discussion of the traumatic event. All the mamas had hushed their crying babies to low whimpers. Many people were down at the altar praising God for sparing them. Some men in the Amen Corner had stopped sniffing and wiping their eyes as well. No one seemed seriously hurt, but many nerves were shaken that day. The preacher himself still aquiver was thankful for all the new converts. He was convinced he had preached a mighty powerful sermon.

But he knew deep down, that God motivated the congregation with the perfectly timed earthquake. Twenty-eight years later, on August 16, 1914, Bennie Hatcher married Minerva Johnson at this same Fountain Campground. They were my husband's grandparents who chose this holy and historic place for their wedding. Every fall, camp meeting services are still held there.

The last of Mother Nature's unusual tantrums was the "Big Blackout," an eclipse of the sun. One eyewitness said, "It was getting so dark that the chickens went to roost while other birds were flying around confused. Then, the dogs stopped barking."

"I was particularly impressed by the unnatural stillness and silence," said Pearl Baker. A while later she said, "I heard from across the field, the workers shouting and praying in fear, and some in panic."

That is what we all felt that day[2].

7. I HEAR YOU KNOCKING

This old story took place in the early 1900s, when life in the South revolved mostly around family and religion. A man who lived in Hancock County was turned out of the church because of something he did; his sin was considered a disgrace. He was very perturbed about the situation. A few months later was the week of revival, and the church had asked the Bishop to come down and preach on Sunday. Since it was a special day, the accused fellow wanted to get in more than ever. But the church would not let him. So, he crawled under the floor boards of the church. Eventually, he reached the place right beneath the Bishop who had stepped down from the pulpit. The Bishop's powerful sermon stirred the congregation that morning, and the "Amen Corner" had begun to shout, "Yes, Lord" and "Amen, Brother."

Meanwhile, the words reached the man—still lying under the church—and, he was greatly moved. When the Spirit touched him, he "got religion," as they say. And then, he began to shout!

"Thank you, dear Jesus! Praise the Lord!" Well, sir, he kept shouting: "Amen, brothers and sisters!"

He shouted so loud and so long, that the Bishop stopped and asked, "Who is that shouting under the floor?"

"That's a man our church won't let in because of a sin he committed."

"Well, let him in, anyway," said the Bishop, very annoyed.

Some of the men dragged him out from under the church, and let him inside, covered with dust and dirt.

What was the terrible sin had he committed? He had taken an unmarried woman fishing with him."[3]

(From my friend, Mr. Paul Farr)

8. CLOSE YOUR EARS

During that same period of time, something happened at a different service. The pastor had started his sermon, and after several minutes, a man stood up in the back of the church.

"Preacher, we can't hear you back here."

There was another man sitting down toward the front. His wife had nudged and strongly encouraged him that they should sit there. Needless to say, this man could hear everything. He stood up, looked at the fellow in the back, and said, "If you can't hear what's being said, then BE THANKFUL!"[4]

(from Mr. Paul Farr)

9. THOSE WERE THE DAYS

My mother was born when dance marathons had people kicking up their heels, *Readers Digest* was first published, and King Tut's tomb was discovered. The year was 1922. Inventions and discoveries included the push-button elevator, lead ethyl gasoline, and vitamin D. By the time she had started to school, everyone felt the throes of the Great Depression. The stock market crashed, people lost their jobs, and everyone suffered in some way. Mama's family left Atlanta to return home to Stockbridge and live with family to make ends meet. Mama and her sister felt like they had moved to the end of the world. Since the roads were dirt, they could no longer roller skate. Although Highway 42 was paved, their mother insisted it was too dangerous. In Stockbridge, life was slow. My mother began...

Before long, we met other children on our street and at church. One of our favorite pastimes was "playing doctor." I called my sister, Mim, short for Miriam, and she called me, Sis. Mim was the doctor, and I was her nurse. Naturally, the children in our neighborhood were our victims, I mean, patients.

When Doctor Mim gave pretend shots with the stem of a broken light bulb, I applied the bandage to stop the bleeding. Once Dr. Mim got a forked stick lodged in a girl's nose, and we could not get it out. She ran home, bleeding and squalling (a good Southern word for crying).

Several phone calls were made from the appalled mothers to our mother. Bad news for us! Our somewhat questionable methods ended our doctoring days.

Meanwhile, we had another pastime; our back yard was the burial site of dead pets, and the cemetery for the neighborhood. The children brought any deceased pet to us. It could be anything—birds, turtles, goldfish, dogs, rabbits or cats—and we laid them to rest in our cemetery. We had a special funeral with Mim as the "official preacher," and I was the "official mourner." After Easter was an especially busy time for us, since many children got ducks, chicks and rabbits. When the pets died, the children brought the little critter to our house.

Next, a string of neighborhood kids formed a funeral procession and walked down the street to our pet cemetery. Preacher Mim started her preaching, praying and hollering for the dearly departed pet. As the mourner, I put an onion inside of a handkerchief and carried it with me. At the appropriate time, I squeezed the onion, and put it near my eyes; believe me, it caused real tears. When all the praying stopped, we carefully buried the pet in a small box.

At the local drugstore, Mim and I could get an occasional ice cream or soda fountain drink. We were allowed to charge the treat to our mother's account. We could even charge a few dollars there...

"Wait a minute," I interrupted, "y'all charged money at a drugstore?"

"That is right."

"Sounds more like a bank to me," I said.

"At the end of the month, our mother paid off the account."

"Wow, those were the days!" I exclaimed. "Maybe so, because we never realized we were lacking anything."

(from my mother)

10. A WHAT?

My grandmother Mon (our mother's mother) had a housekeeper named Babe who worked for her for many years. When Babe's sister died, the family asked her, "Can your cousin Lucy stay with Sister during the wake?"

"Yes, I think so," Babe said.

Meanwhile, Mon went along with Babe and her family to the visitation. (Now, Mon was an avid sun worshiper, so her skin was always dark.) As she mixed and mingled with the aunts, uncles, and cousins, and Babe's family thought Mon was related to them.) They probably wondered why they had not seen her at other gatherings.

That night, Lucy came to take her post. She had been to a wake once, but she had never stayed by the bedside of a departed soul. She sat in a chair near Sister's bed. At first, she was so anxious about being with a dead body; she tried to look around the room to avoid Sister's face. Finally, she peeked through her fingers at her and was awestruck at how her face looked. Not pale at all, but as if she might take a breath at any minute.

As the hours dragged on and on, Lucy felt hot and tired. She pulled her chair over to the open window to cool off. Her eyelids drooped, her head sank to her shoulder as she dozed on and off. She thought she was dreaming when she heard a voice.

As Lucy pried open her eyes, there sat Sister straight up in bed.

"Can I have a banana?" asked Sister.

Lucy jumped out the window.

(from Grandmother Mon)

11. HAS SHE GONE BATTY?

My husband's family knew two ladies, Myrtle and Sadie, who were friends. Sadie's husband had died, and she lived alone. Of course, Sadie was used to her husband handling all the situations that occurred at home.

One night, Sadie returned home. She turned on the lights, and within a few minutes, she saw bats in the room. They were circling throughout the house playing a merry game of tag. (Hmm, this story sounds familiar.)

Naturally, she was terrified and did not know what to do. She phoned Myrtle:

"Myrtle, come quick, come quick."

"What in the world is going on, Sadie?"

"The bats are flying around in my house!"

"Oh, no!"

"Yes, and they are flying at a low '*attitude*.'" (sic)

(from family friends)

12. THE SEVENTH ONE

My daddy was the seventh child, and he was named Jefferson Buchanan Russell. Both of his names were from Russell ancestors. Early on, everyone called him J.B., since his full name was quite a mouthful. When Daddy was about six or seven, he walked with his Mama to Kelley's General Store. Maybe, it was about half a mile from their farmhouse in the country. People were always hanging around there, since it was the only store within miles.

As they got closer, Daddy heard some commotion and hollering like he had never heard before. Then, he caught a glimpse through the trees of someone jumping up and down on something. An old lady was hollering, dancing, and singing about "Some saints come marching in." She yelled like a "fire and brimstone" preacher!

As they got closer, he realized she was on an upholstered hoop cheese box. When they got to the store, Daddy stayed inside for a few minutes. His heart started racing more and more as he heard that lady.

Where was his Mama? He had to get outta that place right that minute, he thought. He lit out and took off running home as fast as he could. His Mama bought a few things, and then realized he was not in the store. She asked around, and finally started home, worried to death. He was sitting on the front steps when she arrived home.

"J.B., why did you leave? I was about worried to death."

"I didn't know what that crazy woman was gonna do; I was scared as a jack rabbit."

"Son, that was Mrs. Shirley, Tom Kelley's mother. She was doing what she usually does."

"What was that?"

"Well, she was preaching; she got religion a while back."

"Oh, I hope that religion don't get me, Mama!"

13. SIMPLER TIMES

In going through an old scrapbook from one of my aunts, I found an envelope marked "Special Delivery." It was addressed to one of my dad's sisters, who was at church camp.

To: "Miss Elizabeth Russell, Camp Smyrna, Conyers, Ga.

The postage amounted to a grand total of "Ten Cents." Plus, the post office had stamped: "postage due <u>five</u> cents." The envelope, was dated July 11, 1936, and contained one small piece of paper, which read:

> *Dear Elizabeth,*
> *Tired of washing dishes. Come home.*
> *Lamar*

Immediately, you could tell Lamar was a true "Russell." Most of the Russell men spoke a few, abrupt words, as well as straight to the point, just like Granddaddy. Plus, their tone was never in the "warm and fuzzy" category.

14. EARLY TO BED, EARLY TO RISE

The scene is a dairy farm owned by my husband's aunt and uncle near White Plains, Georgia, during the early 1940s. Dairy farmers had to be early risers, so generally Uncle Pierce and Aunt Elizabeth went to bed around 9:00 p.m. Milking the cows usually began at 4:00 a.m. (according to a particular cow that always wore a Timex).

One night, Uncle Pierce woke up, elbowed Elizabeth, and asked, "Is it time to get up?"

Not really looking at the clock that closely, she said, "Yes."

He got up, threw on his clothes, scurried out to his truck, and headed out to pick up his helper. As his truck rumbled down the dirt road, he passed by his parents' house, which sat very close to the road. They heard his truck and wondered why he was going by at that time.

They called my aunt.

"Elizabeth, what is going on down there? We just heard Pierce go by."

She replied very sleepily, "Oh, everything is fine; he is heading to pick up Obadiah, like he always does. I've started breakfast, like I usually do," (which meant eggs, bacon, grits, biscuits, jam and coffee).

Ma said, "Well, it is too early for them to go."

Meanwhile, Uncle Pierce had arrived at Obadiah's house and waited several minutes for him to come out. Finally, he came walking slowly out the door.

"Hurry, we are running late."

"Lord, Mister Pierce, I coulda swore (sic) I just got home from the picture show up in Greensboro. I feel like I just laid down."

"Now, come on, Obadiah, it's after 4:00 a.m., and the cows are waiting to be milked."

He got in the truck, and they rode on down to the barn. Much to Uncle Pierce's surprise, no cows were standing out there.

"Hmm, something is wrong."

When he arrived back at the house, my aunt was standing in the kitchen, holding her sides, laughing. She could hardly speak, she had gotten so tickled. The joke continued when Elizabeth called Pierce's parents to explain.

"When I looked at the clock, I was half asleep, and without my glasses it, appeared to be five minutes until four." (Really, it was 11:20 p.m.) "So, Pierce jumped up and got ready," Elizabeth giggled.

Obadiah was happy to go back home to sleep for a while until it was time for the cows to be officially milked. Elizabeth prepared their big breakfast, as usual, about 7:00 a.m., ready for their return. Obviously, the whole family enjoyed teasing Uncle Pierce about his mistake for the rest of his life.

15. THEM THAR HILLS

Way up yonder in them thar hills lived Grandpa and Grandma. Everyone was either related to them or had known them forever. Rarely, did they set foot off the property and go to town. They had been married a long, long time, and eventually Grandpa died. Alpha was hired to live with Grandma and take care of her.

Well, after a while, Grandma's mind began to fail. She became more and more confused. She kept thinking that Grandpa was still living. Nothing could convince her otherwise.

One day, she fell and broke her wrist. She refused to leave the house to get medical help.

Her son called.

"Mama, you have to go with the policeman, so he can take you to the doctor."

"I can't leave the house without Grandpa; he won't know where I am," Grandma firmly stated.

"Mama, you can leave him a note."

"Son, that won't help…you know that your Grandpa can't read."

Apparently, Alpha talked and talked to Grandma. She convinced her to leave: "Now, my sister Omega can stay with Grandpa."

"Are you sure she won't leave him?"

"No, she will stay right here. Alpha and Omega were the first and last helpers she had.

(as told by my friend)

16. DOC IS OUT

Meanwhile, in another small town during that same time, a lady's five-year-old grandson was spending the night with her. Late that night he was burning up with fever, but she hesitated about calling the local doctor. Finally, she got so worried, she called.

"Doctor, I am very sorry to call you this late, but little James' fever keeps going up."

Dr. Dill was very tired and did not want to get dressed to go out again. (Doctors used to make house calls in small towns.)

"Yes, Mrs. Smith, sorry to hear he is not well, but it IS very late."

"But, doc, you just don't understand how sick he is."

"I'll tell you what. Give him two aspirins, put him back to bed, and he'll be better in the morning," answered the exhausted doctor.

"Well, I never," as she furiously slammed down the phone.

She and her husband immediately took little James to the hospital emergency room where he was treated. A few weeks later, the same doctor called Mrs. Smith.

"Hello, Mrs. Smith, my refrigerator stopped working."

"Oh, is that right?" she asked. "Yes, I am trying to locate your son Bill to fix it."

"I don't know where he is, but I'll tell you what to do. Just open the refrigerator door, throw in two aspirins, and it will be running by morning."

(from my husband)

17. NOT SO APPETIZING

Warning: may gag.

Sarah, a lady our family knew, went to visit her dear friend in another state. They had known each other many years and were very close. In fact, Sarah called her friend "Aunt Penny," even though they were not related.

When lunchtime came, Aunt Penny brought out steaming bowls of vegetable soup and cornbread. After a few minutes, Sarah remarked, "Goodness, this soup is absolutely delicious; it tastes exactly like your mother used to make."

"Well, dear, as a matter of fact it IS her soup," replied Aunt Penny.

"Oh, gosh, I thought she died."

"She did…10 years ago."

"Oh…" Sarah gasped, choking on her soup.

(from a family friend)

Chapter 2

NOT SO FAR BACK

(Thank heavens, we are worn out
with the old people stories!)

1. MAMA AND DADDY S FIRST BROOD

After Mama and Daddy got married, they decided to raise some baby chicks.

"I can get some wood and build them a little chicken crate to live in," Daddy said.

So, he constructed a little home for them. He bought some biddies (baby chicks) at the hardware store and brought them home to their new digs. He put the biddies in the crate along with chicken feed and little saucers of water for them.

As the weeks passed, the chicks ate, drank, and pooped. Their crate got pretty messy as their poopy feet stepped in and out of the water. Mama cleaned out the crate, gave them new water, and fed them. Each week they grew bigger and bigger. Since Mama and Daddy were proud of their little brood, Mama invited some friends to come see them.

A few days later, a couple stopped by; Mama was anxious to show them their pride and joy.

"Oh, goodness, what is wrong with them?" the lady asked. "They are walking funny!"

"Yes, there is a slight problem. J.B. did not figure in the growth factor so they are too tall to walk on their feet. They move around on their knees," Mama giggled.

"Oh, we see now," said the couple, trying not to laugh.

"Please don't mention it to J.B."

Mama knew he would never admit his mistake; he would probably blame the chicks for growing so big.

2. UNCLE JAKE

Mama, Daddy, Uncle Jake, and Aunt Mim went on a trip to the beach in Panama City, Florida. (Mim was my mama's only sister.) You see, Uncle Jake had never seen the ocean and was stunned by the clear waters of the Gulf of Mexico. They went down to the boat docks where the fishing charter boats brought in fish at the end of the day. The crewmen hung heavy ropes of fish down from the boat tops, where everyone could view their catches for the day. And, Jake was speechless when he saw hundreds of red snapper, grouper, sea bass, and more strung up. And he was totally awestruck seeing fish weighing 30 to 40 pounds. He was able to get a couple of large fish from one of the boat's captain.

My daddy asked, "Jake, what do you want to do with the fish?"

"Well, I'd like to take them home."

"How?" asked my daddy.

"Let's just wrap them in newspaper, and lay them in the boot of your car." (Boot was a common name for the trunk back then.)

"I reckon we can try." I know my Daddy was thinking to himself, *This is a predicament...* but he did not want to disappoint Jake.

"Just wait till the fellows in Stockbridge see these things," said Jake.

As the day went on, the temperatures kept rising. Naturally, those fish began to smell to high heaven. (Cars did not have air conditioners then.)

Mama and Aunt Mim whispered to each other, "Fellows, we hate to say this, but we are getting sick from the terrible odor."

"Just put some napkins over your nose; that will help," suggested Jake.

"J.B., we have to do something," Mama said.

Daddy remained silent. He did NOT want to make a decision. Uncle Jake did NOT want to give up his prize possessions, the very stinky fish. Mama and Mim did NOT want to throw up. In the car, or elsewhere.

"Jake, what do you think?" asked J.B.

"Oh, okay, okay, pull over." J.B. maneuvered the car off the steamy pavement.

Sadly and slowly, Jake got out and opened the boot. He heaved up the stinkers and slung them into a swampy ditch. That was a tale of tails, and no one wants to re-tell that stinker.

And our parents always said we did such crazy things!

3. DADDY AND BOOTS

Many years later, when Daddy was a grown man, he was still stopping at Kelley's store. Many folks heading past the store turned left onto Elliott Road. Going down that dirt road was a steep hill until you reached Walnut Creek, where it leveled off. And, climbing back up the hill from the creek to the store was especially rough on the cars back then. Most cars ran hot and had to stop at the general store to use his well. Everyone would draw up water in the bucket and pour it into the radiator to cool the car or truck off.

Daddy and his right-hand man, Boots, were driving out Highway 20 in his '29 Model Chevrolet. They had gone down the road past Walnut Creek to do some work. Heading back up, sure enough, his Chevy ran hot. Back then, radiators easily overheated. They puttered to Kelly's store, where he drew water up from the well and refilled the radiator. Mrs. Shirley was still preaching and shouting. By now, she had begun to sew a red dot on white handkerchiefs that stood for Jesus' blood.

Daddy warned Boots, "When we get to the store, Mrs. Shirley will ask you to say a Bible verse."

"Mister J.B., I don't know a verse in the Bible by heart," replied Boots.

"Just say, 'Jesus wept,' and she will give you a Jesus' handkerchief."

So he did, and she did. Then came her, "God Bless you!" for Boots.

Then, Daddy said his verse, she handed him his handkerchief with the red dot, and "God Blessed me!" Daddy said.

After they had passed her rituals, the Chevy had cooled off, and they started back home. Daddy remembered Mrs. Kelley, from years ago, and she was still a'preaching.

Chapter 3

KNEE HIGH TO A GRASSHOPPER

(When I Was a Kid...)

1. THOSE FABULOUS, LONG SUMMERS

Summertime was wonderful. My good friend Joice and I walked uptown barefoot on a dirt road in the spring. It was the back way to town. By June, our soles were "tough" and ready for summer. Toughness was needed since I had a past history of stepping on sharp rocks, bees, and once, a burning cigarette butt when I was a tenderfoot. Joice lived down the street on the corner literally within shouting distance. I yelled when I was ready to meet her on the corner to walk to town, and vice versa.

Our eighth grade English teacher, Miss Nell Newman, lived halfway between us, much to her dismay. The year we were in her class, she chose both of us for parts in the school program.

She said in front of the class, "I know these two can certainly speak up, since I have listened to their shouting from one corner to the other."

Our favorite place to go was Ward Drug Company. We sat on the stools at the counter to place our order. They had the best freshly squeezed lemonade, yummy milkshakes, chocolate hunkies, and the best ice cream in the world. We were regulars. Occasionally, we spotted and picked up a small green snake on our way to town. Once we wrote our initials on one with a magic marker. (Later, the Department of Natural Resources adopted our method of tagging reptiles). Then, we released the little serpent back into the ditch and hoped to find him again on another day.

One day, I took a green snake into Ward's Drugstore and placed it on the counter. When I stretched it straight out, it laid completely still. Almost like it was trained. When the lady came to take our order, she was startled and jumped back. Then, she said, "It's not real, is it?"

"Yes, ma'am, it is."

"Oh, but it is lying so still."

"Yes, ma'am."

She kept repeating, "Whew! I sure am glad it is just a rubber snake."

We kept giggling, and saying, "But, Ma'am, it IS real!"

After we got our order, we practically ran out the door, to keep from busting out laughing. (In the South, we "busted'" and never "burst" out laughing, no matter how grammatically incorrect it was.)

On our trek home, we let the snake go back into ditch. We did not stop laughing all the way back, retelling each other the details of our tale with a tail. And, how the lady was fooled! This was one of those 'you had to be there' for it to be funny. The retelling falls a little flat, but I had to include it.

2. FLEW THE COOP

As a family of six, our parents were very resourceful in many ways. We wore hand-me-downs, hand-me-overs, or whatever was passed in any direction. Plus, our industrious Mama made many of our clothes; man, she could pump the pedal on that Singer and just fly on those seams! I always loved what she made because often we could pick out our own material.

In the summer, the folks on Daddy's mail route left big brown paper bags of corn, tomatoes, beans, banana peppers, and peas next to their mailboxes for him to pick up. What a blessing for us! The bad part we remember was we had to shuck the corn and shell the beans and peas before we could go to the swimming pool. We sat on the screen porch fooling with those beans until our fingernails turned greenish. Not to mention the lucky one who encountered a nice, chubby, white grub gnawing on the corn. Yuck!

I am not complaining. My parents, like many others, worked extremely hard to give us what we needed and many extras. Once, I remember Mama came driving down in the back yard in one of our big, long, old cars.

She yelled, "Ya'll, come on down behind your daddy's shop."

Uh-oh, what's going on this time? I wondered. She had never driven a car back there.

"When I open up the trunk," (which was at least 6 feet long) "we will catch the chickens," she instructed. Well, suh (as they say in the South), she unlocked the boot, and such a multitude of chickens exploded upward that the shadows of their bodies and feathered wings briefly darkened the sky. We were slightly stunned. And horrified.

When they landed, they went north, east, south, and west. Next, they flew up, and they flew down. We ran, and they ran; then, they ran, and we ran. We were not sure if we or the chickens were the pursuers or the pursued. Many neighbors came from every direction when they heard all the noises and loud squawking, and that was the sound we kids were making. Since I was a fast runner, I could have caught a lot of chickens. Only one itsy, bitsy problem: the terror of grabbing a live fowl with its sharp beak and its reddish, icky, webbed feet was very scary. No telling what bodily damage the angry critter could inflict.

Eventually, most of the chickens were corralled, but I am positive some escaped. Everyone in the neighborhood kept talking about how much they enjoyed fresh, fried chicken that week. I don't remember Mama ever bringing home live chickens again. I think I was still in counseling, anyway.

3. THE O.K. CORRAL

My brother and I liked riding ponies and horses. One day, Uncle Charles and Aunt Elizabeth called about our coming out to their farm to ride a new horse. We decided to ride together, against our uncle's advice. Within a minute of climbing into the saddle, that horse became alive. You have never seen such wild bucking in your life. We hung on as long as we could, which was a grand total of maybe five seconds, or less; then, we were catapulted sky high, it seemed. The next thing everyone heard was two dull thuds and many ouches. Those were the sounds Leon and I made when our young bodies collided with the hard, rocky ground.

Around farms and corrals, people always say, "if you fall off a horse, you should immediately get back on it." Okay, maybe that is true. But, you see, we were bucked off. That is a horse of a different color, so to speak. If anyone tells you to get back on a bucking bronco, he has rocks in his head.

4. HE SAID HE COULD

That same day, a young fellow had come out to Uncle Charles' house to get a job. Uncle Charles wanted to hire him if things worked out. He showed him around the farm and asked what he knew about country life.

Uncle Charles asked, "Son, do you know how to drive a tractor?"

"Uh…yessir, I know how."

"All right, then. Get on that tractor and drive down the road a bit."

The young man climbed up onto the old tractor, fumbled around, and found the key ignition. He cranked up the engine. (Southerners do not "start up" an engine.) He shifted some gears around and proceeded to drive. He immediately took a quick right turn and plowed directly into the shed attached to the barn.

My uncle, my daddy, Leon, and I were watching in utter disbelief. Within seconds, he had ripped off the roof and totally destroyed the shed. You can only imagine the sound of boards splintering, and pieces flying and crashing everywhere. Loud screeching and whining blasted our ears as the rusty, tin roof folded up like a giant accordion; the wild tractor smashed through like a demolition bulldozer. The terrified fellow was pelted with debris as it tumbled down. Nothing was left, but scattered planks, bits of wood, crushed tin, bent nails, and sawdust blowing everywhere.

Well, some things were left: the banged-up tractor, the fellow, and us.

All of us still stood there motionless with our mouths hanging open in shock. At first. Then, we shut our mouths quickly and covered our faces to fend off all the dust and debris: A bad day for the fellow and a worse day for our uncle.

Finally, Uncle Charles said, "Well, young man, come back next week."

"Are you going to hire me?"

"No, but you will rebuild my shed."

5. SCAREDY CAT

Once I spent the night with Uncle Charles and Aunt Elizabeth where we rode horses. They lived in a large, spooky, two-story house with a long staircase leading to an unused, second floor. They did not want us to go up there and explore. I never knew why, except they said it was dirty and dusty. Maybe they had skeletons in the closet, but we never got to spend enough time to find out. At bedtime, I heard mysterious noises, but finally drifted off to sleep.

The next morning I got up and began to get dressed. When I slipped my right foot into my shoe, my toes met the most horrid surprise; a wiggling something with legs…many, many legs. Absolutely terrified, I threw off my shoe and watched a GIANT SPIDER crawl out. I starting hollering! (In the South, we hollered more than we screamed.) My mind goes blank as to what happened next.

When I went home, I was telling my family about the spider episode.

"Was he hairy?" someone asked.

"I don't know what his name was…I was too scared, to ask."

6. WHAT IS CAMP MEETING?

Camp meeting is much more than a place, time, or gathering of people. Rarely can anyone describe it in 25 words or less! When we were growing up, camp meeting meant playing in the clear, cold water of the spring, playing ball within the huge square, eating ice-cold watermelon, sitting at a long table filled with delicious food with our family and friends, going down to the store to buy ice cream and all sorts of candies, and singing the wonderful camp meeting songs. Truly, a time you never forgot! It was a week of fellowship with family, relatives, and old friends you met there as children. Sleeping in the rustic cabins was so much fun with open windows (no screens), wood shavings on the floor, a heavy cloth curtain as the bedroom door, and sharing the rooms with family, cousins, and friends. Church services were held in the big, shingle-roof tabernacle, and outstanding ministers and choirs came to preach and worship in music with us.

It began in the 1800s as people gathered after the harvesting of crops. They loaded down their horse or mule drawn wagons with food, pots, pans, clothing, blankets, and sundry items to camp out for at least two weeks. They met near a cool spring and brought along their cows, and chickens, which provided milk, eggs, and fried chicken. The dogs tagged along like members of the family. Usually, the families gathered at the same place each year. Early on, they gathered brush and small trees to construct their shelters, or arbors. They settled down at night under the beautiful stars and told stories of their ancestors. The children loved these camping out adventures and grew up in this great tradition.

In those days, circuit preachers were always scouring the countryside in search of a group of people to whom they could preach. They found the places where the campers met yearly; this tradition evolved into a phrase known as "camp meeting." These preachers were happy and anxious to preach to any gathering of people. Actually, these folks were strong, traditionally Protestant people. The camp meeting we attend is sponsored by the Methodist Church in McDonough, and is named Shingleroof Campground. One of the great traditions has been to cook an abundance of delicious food...fresh turnip greens, corn, peas, fried meat, squash, okra, and cornbread or freshly baked biscuits. Plus ice cold water dipped up from the spring, or good ole sweet tea. No preacher in his right mind could ever turn down a feast like that.

As time passed, camp meeting goers used tents instead of arbors. They became known as "tenters," and usually set up their tents side by side in the shape of a big square. In the middle grassy area, a permanent, large arbor was built for the preacher to deliver his messages. The people sat on the ground or on benches, singing the grand ole hymns of redemption and faith. The arbor became a tabernacle built of freshly hewn boards of oak or pine. The roof was covered with boards and handmade shingles. Wooden benches were built, and the ground was laid with freshly cut wood shavings and sawdust.

7. SOUNDS FISHY

(Doesn't smell much better either! Look here, I have several fish tales to tell…skip this section if you are not crazy about fish or stories about fish)

My earliest remembrances of fishing were probably down at Jackson Lake. (Atlanta folks now call it Lake Jackson, bless their hearts.) At that time, it was quite a trek to get to the rustic cabins. Once you left the main highway, you bumped over rocks and roots on a dirt path, almost qualifying as a road. Overgrown tree branches slapped you in the face if you dared to roll down your window. As we snaked around through tangled vines and blackberry bushes, we saw signs displaying the nicknames of cabins. Not artistic signs, but akin to what a kid would slap on a ragged piece of wood. One that puzzled us for a while was 'Weunslikeit.' Every time we passed it, we wondered what it said. To us it was foreign. Finally, we got it: "We-uns-like-it."

Our Russell family, and our close friends, the Fosters, were invited down to the Harris' place to fish. Their cabin was up on a hill, which sloped down to the water; their free-range chickens scratched and wandered everywhere. This was way before the "free range" terminology became cool. Five or six of us grabbed cane poles and worms and ran down to the lake. Just the kids. We excitedly baited our hooks and swung our lines out until the corks went ker-plunk. Back then, "corks" were actually made from cork trees; later, they became "floats" made from plastic. Yes, I know; everything is made of plastic now.

Meanwhile, the chickens continued scratching the dirt all up and down the hill searching for bugs and worms. As they approached us, the "little smartie pants" chickens spied our bait. You see, when you are fishing with a cane pole, you sling your line backward and then forward toward the water. You don't need to look back because no one but a fool would be standing behind you. Meanwhile the chickens kept their eyes glued on the hooked worms sliding up and down the hill on our sling backs.

Unknown to us, the feathery thieves scurried back and forth, up and down trying to capture our bait. We were clueless to their antics since we were yakking, watching our corks, catching fish, and re-baiting our hooks. Just having a great time! Then, Bobby Foster, the oldest son, slung his line back, and tried to swing it forward. It would not budge. Instantly, our ears were blasted with the worst screeching, squawking and gagging noise.

Our heads swirled instantly toward Bobby's direction as we mindlessly dropped our poles. As he was struggling with his very heavy line, he was shocked when he looked back. The catch of the day...A CHICKEN! We all started hollering, and scampering toward them (Bobby and his chicken).

Our parents, hearing all the commotion, came running down the bank dodging the other free rangers. After much ado, Mr. Harris gloved up and freed the very ruffled and indignant chicken. The chicken concluded to herself, "That is a rough way to get one measly worm."

Later on, our families (the Fosters and the Russells) bought a cabin together across the cove from the Harris' place. I don't think they ever invited us back. We really never knew why.

Chapter 4
TEN YEARS OLD

1. PICNICKING FISH

When we were 10 or so, our group of friends formed a hiking club, later known as the "Adventurers Club." The members were Betty, Lynda, Pam, Joice, Kathi, and I. We packed our picnic lunches and struck out toward Conyers Road. We cut through the back of a neighborhood not far from Lynda Reeves house. She knew the streets and where to cross to reach a small pond.

We skipped a few rocks in the pond and headed toward the beautiful woods filled with oaks, pines, and maples. Following a little creek, we saw a huge water moccasin, down in the water. Undeterred, we kept exploring until we found an inviting spot where we played in the water and ate our lunch sitting on the mossy banks and larger rocks.

After several trips down there, we shortened the name of our club to the "A" Club.

One time, I decided to fish with part of my leftover lunch. I reached in my pocket, and pulled out my string with a hook. Doesn't every Girl Scout come prepared? Sure enough, I caught a tiny fish using the most unusual bait ever...a bite of a dill pickle.

Once, we proudly led our mothers down to see our wonderful oasis. When they realized how isolated and how deep in the woods we were, they were less than happy. They forbade our "A" Club to ever go again.

That ended that.

2. THIS IS A GOOD UN

If you hang around, I have a really exciting fish tale for you.

One summer afternoon, Daddy asked me to go fishing with him; even though I was a girl, I was his fishing buddy. We stopped to pick up our live bait—worms and crickets—and headed out to a man's pond way out in the sticks. Daddy usually had a saying that matched most situations. For fishing, he had several, but I remember, "Never stand up in a boat."

Finally, we located the place and met the fellow at his swampy-looking, small pond. The three of us carefully stepped down into his small john boat, which was a tight fit. Not only was my dad a tall man, but we had to load our gear and bait. After we got settled, I thought to myself, *Gosh, we are sitting very low on the water...* Nautical language, meaning the sides of the boat were only several inches above the water.

We fished for a little while. Suddenly, a large head shot up over the side of the boat; a gigantic water moccasin wanted to get into the boat with us. Instantly, we all jumped straight up, and the little boat rocked violently. It was all we could do to keep our balance and not fall into the water. Just the thought of going into the water with that monster was terrifying.

That shrewd serpent swam underneath our boat and popped his head up over the other side.

Wham! Wham!

My dad struck at him with the paddle. Again, that rascal (the snake, not my dad) slipped underneath the boat, trying its best to slither over the top edge. Then, Daddy whacked again, either wounding or killing it. That is all I remember about that fishing trip. If we caught any fish that day, it paled in comparison with that moccasin attack. And, as I grew up, that event ranked high on the list as one of the most terrifying times of my life. My dad never said another word about the "no standing up in the boat" rule. Plus, there was never any mention of ever returning to that swampy pond again.

Lastly, one point of clarification has to be added here. It was not that we were bad Southerners by not letting that vile snake go for a little ride. As you know, we are famous for being very hospitable. The fact was we, did not have a life jacket in the snake's size. And, you could NOT ride in a boat without one that fit you; that rule was written in STONE.

3. PLAYING BALL

My brother and I spent hours playing ball with our friends. As a tomboy, I received many bruises and cuts which accompanied this pastime. Possibly, my discombobulated recollections and distorted memories stemmed from significant blows to my head from baseballs, footballs, tennis balls, and the hard ground. At camp meeting once, we were playing softball; I was the runner on third base. At the crack of the bat, I turned to run home when a line drive (from my teammate) knocked me on my forehead. I was out cold. Some of my teammates ran and summoned Grandmother Russell for help.

As I blinked awake, I looked upward and she said, "I don't know why you always want to play ball with the boys!"

If I waited for words of sympathy, I would still be lying there until this very day. Our family's dialogue was not chock full of sympathetic words or encouragement. Fortunately, their spirit of toughness and resiliency eventually gave me a strong will and disposition.

4. PETS AND SUCH

Growing up I always had pets. In the house, I raised snails, turtles, guppies, and goldfish. One particular turtle I had was named Harold Oliver; he crawled under the refrigerator and never returned. Also, I named my snail families: The red one was named Rhode Island Reds, and the black one was named Boston Blackies. The problem was, those snails multiplied like rabbits.

I loved puppies, but our parents' main rule was, "No dogs inside the house." When I got a puppy, it had to stay on the back porch. Of course, it whimpered all night. Someone said to put a ticking clock with it to keep it company, but the puppy just used it as a fire hydrant. And, it did not seem that comforted. I had several outside dogs: Giblet was a small Heinz 57 variety; Cinnamon was also a mix, and her name matched her color; Skeeter was a Cocker Spaniel; Prissy I and Prissy II were both collies from my friend Joice.

Our neighbors were not happy with our canines. If I had a puppy, it loved to go next door, bite into the sheets on the clothesline and swing back and forth. When it tired of that, he enjoyed poking at the tiny gold fish they had in a special pond. My neighbors failed to see the humor of teeth marks on their sheets and their gold fish being terrified by puppy paws.

5. GRASS MAN

Also, there was an eccentric man who lived right down the street from us. He sat most of the time in his yard staring and picking up blades of grass. Sometimes, he put clumps of grass up in a tree. We named him, "Grass Man."

We had to walk past his hovel every day since it was on our way home. My dad said his place had actually been a chicken coop before he lived there. We were so scared of him, we ran by his home. I don't think he ever said anything to us, just stared. Probably harmless. He did odd things, like he spray-painted his old boots silver. This situation stayed the same for a long time.

Finally, one day, I was in the front yard watering the flowers with my back toward the street. An eerie sensation went over me, and I sensed someone was watching me. I turned around, and there was Grass Man standing in our yard staring at me. I threw down the hose and went flying into the house.

I ran in and hollered, "Daddy, Daddy, Grass Man is out there." I was petrified.

Daddy grabbed his shotgun and headed out the front door. We did not hear any shots, but he must have threatened him. Grass Man never stopped at our house again.

6. SALTY TALE

My lifelong attraction to birds has not necessarily been shared by the birds. As a child I ran around the yard with a salt shaker trying to catch them. You see, Mama had said, "You can catch a bird if you sprinkle salt on its tail." The birds would have no part of it. Mama never dreamed we would take her advice literally, and I'm sure she wondered why the salt shakers were always low on salt.

My brother was also involved with the bird-catching schemes. We propped a square cardboard box upside down on a forked stick. We tossed potato peelings under the box as bait (maybe Mama had just peeled some potatoes). Next, we attached a very long string to the stick and hid behind a bush across the yard. When a little bird hopped underneath the box, we jerked the string. Our box clumsily fell down only to scare the bird away. So, no luck there.

As I got older, my fascination with birds continued. I could hardly wait for a bluebird to visit my new birdhouse. I was so thrilled one day when I spied a little head in the opening. Every time I passed by the window, I peeked out to see the bluebird.

Then, I realized something unusual; the bird had not moved all day long. When I gazed straight ahead, I could see my feathered friend; if I turned my head to the side, the bird's head moved, too. Hmm...

As it turned out, my so-called bird was actually a speck stuck on my glasses. Just my luck!

7. MAKING MONEY

We got a quarter a week for our allowance, so I was always thinking of ways to make extra money. I made potholders from loopers that I wove on a loom and sold them to relatives and neighbors. I collected glass drink bottles and got 2 cents apiece at the grocery store. Grandmother paid a nickel for a small bucket of pecans. Joice and I picked peaches at Cap Welch's orchard, but don't know if we got paid.

Daddy owned an apartment house and duplex. He paid me five dollars to cut the grass. It was a hard yard to cut since part of it included a gravel driveway littered with scattered coke bottle caps, broken pieces of coat hangers, nails, and junk. My worse injury was when my lawn mower hit a small piece of a hanger and drove it into my shin. I still sport the round scar. This was my tattoo of the 1960s. Mama paid Leon and me extra to wash the windows on the inside and out. Eventually, I saved up $30 and bought my first bicycle, which was the most perfect color of purple. What a reward for all my hard work!

8. AN UNUSUAL NAME

We did not know much about politics when we were young. Later on, we still did not know much, but we heard about a man with the most unusual name: Zell. Early in his career, Zell Miller held a rally up in north Georgia near his hometown of Young Harris. He had hired a country singer to perform. When the fundraiser ended, he gave the singer a check for $150. As she headed home, she passed through Hiawassee and saw the bank on which the check was written. She stopped at the bank and went inside. She approached the bank teller, "Ma'am, I am from out of town. I just sang at an event for this man named Zell Miller."

"Oh, I see," replied the teller.

"I am not sure about this check since I didn't know him, so I decided I should cash the check before I left the area."

"Honey, don't worry about the check being good…it is signed by my husband."

(True story told by Zell Miller, former Governor of Georgia; we became friends with him at a little café in Hayesville, North Carolina.)

9. PICTURE SHOW

Of course, I always saved for the picture show (movies). Going to the show was a tremendous thrill to me; no other experience was quite like it. A quarter covered admission, a Coca-Cola, and bag of popcorn.

My friends and I shuffled and walked into the semi-darkness squinting through dusty shafts of light and blurry shapes of people's heads, tattered seats and a lit-up exit sign. As we breathed in all the scents of buttered popcorn, melting chocolate, and sweaty kids, we stumbled along, bumping in to each other and giggling. Our tennis shoes stuck to the floor coated with countless spilled drinks and pieces of candy as we searched for a few seats together. Plus, we made sure to avoid the broken or torn seats. In a broken one, your body slumped forward, or sank horizontally to the side, or back. Not acceptable.

Then, *CLICK!* All the lights went out. Pitch dark! I started really giggling at the thought of sitting on someone, which I had done before. Within a minute or two, available light from the cartoons and previews helped us find some vacant spots where we collapsed with our Cokes, candy, and popcorn. I could hardly contain my excitement as the old reel clicked and clicked, and the show started.

What an amazing world of sights and sounds where I became totally absorbed in the picture. It was a magical time for me! And that same thrill returns whenever I enter a movie theater now.

Chapter 5
DAD RULES

1. GRUFF OR NOT, HERE WE COME

Believe it or not, my dad was very strict, gruff, and stubborn exactly like his own dad. However, he did take us to do some wonderful things. When I was about 10 years old, my mother and dad took me out for a special night. We went to the Barn Dinner Theater in south Atlanta. That was a big deal then, just like going to the Fox Theater was a very special occasion. Since it was around Christmastime, we enjoyed all the houses outlined with Christmas lights, and luminous trees glowing through the windows. Everything was just wonderful. We had made our reservations, and they expected everyone to arrive early to eat before the play began; the waiters had to clear the tables quickly and get out of the way so everyone could see the play.

My mother said, "J, it seems longer than usual; I think we are lost."

"Naw, we ain't lost," he responded gruffly. (Who does that sound like?)

We continued to drive up and down many streets and through endless neighborhoods.

"J, I believe we are going in circles," she said.

I cringed in the back seat knowing exactly where this conversation was headed.

"Naw, we're fine."

"Well, I hate to say it, but we've driven by that same Christmas tree two times," my mother continued. Man, I **hated** for her to say it, too. Knowing my Dad, who was never wrong, or lost, probably thought to himself, *Someone has moved the theater.* We did not have phones with directions or GPS in those days. Of course, Daddy did not stop for help.

But by the grace of the Good Lord, we found the place. I don't know who was more relieved, me, Mama, or the Good Lord. By now it was a few minutes till showtime. Hurriedly, we were rushed to our seats as the waiters literally slammed our plates of food on our table. We took a few bites, and the lights dimmed.

When I heard the voices, and the stage lights came up, my mind was spirited away. In center stage, the costumed actors were so close, I could almost touch them. I was in total awe again as my whole being melted into the moments of a newer magical place.

2. DEALS

My daddy loved to get bargains, or "deals" as he called them. We came home at times to see a different vehicle in the front or back yard. Once, it was an old black car that looked like it was used in the show, *The Untouchables.* It started with a push button (before their popularity brought them back in the 2000s). And, I actually used it to teach my nieces how to drive. I remember a $100 truck our dad bought. We decided to take it for a little spin around the block.

I will stop the story here, so I can add more details from my brother Leon. My two sisters, Dianne, Marilyn and I had gone down to visit our brother Leon and his wife Linda in Gulf Shores, Alabama. While we were sitting around yakking and laughing, I hoped to get details about different stories from all of them. At least, that was my secret plan to add depth to my stories. I began telling my brother this story about the truck.

He and I took the truck around the block. When we reached the stoplight, he pressed down on the brakes. No brakes! We sailed through the light and had an accident.

"You were the driver," I added.

"No, it wasn't me; I have no memory of that truck," he firmly stated.

"I could have sworn it was you," I replied.

"Nope, not me. I have never had a wreck."

Gosh, I don't think I know anyone else who has never had a car accident. Well, somebody and I had a wild ride in that piece of a truck. And, after much contemplation later, a thought hit me squarely in my noggin. I guess that should not be a surprise; everything else has struck me there. May be the driver was my Dad. I will ask him one day in heaven when he and I are fishing in the Jordan River around Jerusalem. By then, he will know the best fishing spots.

Returning to the scene, after going through the light, the truck swerved left, hit the curb, bumped upward onto the grassy median and was abruptly stopped by a large oak tree. This unplanned meeting of the tree and truck occurred about 1965 or 1966, when I was 15 or 16 years old. That regal truck was a goner, but luckily the rider only suffered severe memory loss. And speaking of luck, we did not hit an oncoming car before the tree stepped in front of us. Although Keys Ferry Road was a main thoroughfare, there were fewer vehicles on the roads then. If someone wrote an accident report, it is now stored in the very old and very cold case files.

3. LITTLE SIGN

Many years ago, Daddy bought a sign to hang up in our house. It said, "Today is the tomorrow you worried about yesterday."

I admit, you do have to don your thinking cap to understand its meaning. We assumed the sign was for our mother. She was a constant worrier, which is not an uncommon thing. Daddy said, "Ninety percent of what she worried about, never happened." That did not discourage her in the least. She continued her pattern of obsessive worrying to the utmost degree.

I remember telling her, "Mama, when I grow up, I am not going to worry like you do."

So, I changed the word to "concerned." I admit I get very concerned. She used a technique I called "pre-worry." If someone in our family was getting married, she got nervous about the event eight months in advance. I think it was her way of considering all the details that could go wrong so that she could head off the mistakes at the pass. That was a good idea in one sense. She wanted things to be perfect, as well as us, which was not a good idea.

Chapter 6
COLLEGE

1. THE JITNEY

Since there were four children in our family, it was very hard for my dad to buy cars for us. He worked at least three jobs as it was, but growing up, I was in my own world and did not even know that. Many things, our parents did not discuss with us. I never had a car in high school, just like most of my friends. Our friend Joice had a blue Mustang, but she was the only one I remember…but don't hold me accountable.

Finally, I was able to get a car my junior year in college. My dad was still getting special deals on cars. It was a Ford Fairlane, and lasted about a year or so. Some people said the problem was its make, Ford. FORD stood for "Fix Or Repair Daily."

I said, "No, that's not true. It has to be fixed every two to three weeks, not daily." So there! Some people think they know everything.

*(Chosen "Best" story in the "Short and Sweet" category.)

2. LONG TRIP HOME

Two of my college friends, Bonnie and Gayle, were with me as we headed home from college on a Friday afternoon. We were driving the back roads since interstates were scarce during the 1960s in south Georgia. We were so thirsty, and there were not any gas stations or places to stop.

Finally, we spied a small, old store off the road. We called that sort of place "a greasy spoon" back then. And, it was. When we entered through a ragged screen door, we spied the icky, yukky strips of flypaper covered in flies and other victims. The windows were coated with dust and grim, and the plastic tablecloths were smitten with crumbs and drops of ketchup. It was a lovely establishment. We ordered a coca cola, anyway. Our throats were so parched, we thought the waitress would never bring our drinks. The second she sloshed our smudged glasses on the table, we guzzled the fizzy liquid down. Gayle looked at Bonnie's glass, and then at Bonnie.

Then, with a deadpan look, Gayle asked, "Bonnie, how many legs does a raisin have?"

Bonnie's face stared back, "Uh, uh, what do you mean?"

"Look at your glass."

We all saw a roach submerged in her Coke. Our dear friend turned pale and almost fainted. Horrible as the situation was, Gayle and I could not stop laughing.

Chapter 7

AIRLINE HOSTESS

1. MOTORING ALONG

Then, Daddy got me another car. This was a better model; it had a real engine made by Mattel. I drove it to Memphis when I started flying for Southern Airways. Having a car was indispensable since we had to cover a flight on a moment's notice. We were brand new flight attendants with reserve status, which meant we were "on call." Two other attendants and I lived together to share expenses for an apartment, bills, and food. When Scheduling called, they could have a flight for us leaving very soon. We had to hurriedly dress, have a bag packed, and race to the airport about 10 minutes away. We timed each other to see how fast we could get ready if they called.

You will never ever guess what happened. I began to have trouble... that's right...with my car. I took it to a service station down the road. The mechanic worked on it a while, and I assumed (first mistake) it was fixed. For the next flight, my trip departed in the afternoon, and my old jitney worked fine. When I returned on my morning flight, I walked out to my car in the parking lot. It would not crank. I called my mechanic, and he picked me up and took me home. Again, he worked on it and thought the problem was solved. It got to the point that half the time, the mechanic drove me to the airport; he was the "Original Uber Driver" (in the 70s) before the real Uber was started. The other times, my heap cranked, and I drove myself. My roommates were usually out on their flights, so no one was home to drive or pick me up. Everyone at my house, the other mechanics at the station, and the airline folks all flipped coins every time I had a flight somewhere. They placed bets as to whether my car would crank or not. Some folks retired on all the correct bets they made. Not me. I kept working to pay for my grand jitney's numerous overnights at the Hotel "Greasy Service Station."

The Sherlock Holmes in me finally got a break, so to speak, in the case. I discovered the mystery of my car's pattern: It did not crank in the morning (without its coffee), but in the afternoon after "High Tea," no problem. I did not reveal to anyone that I had deciphered the mystery of my ride, just in case I was wrong. Neither did my Memphis mechanic. We knew it liked to sleep late, but we did not know WHY.

So, my Dad gave it to my Uncle Webbie (Welborn), who always went to the store in the afternoon. Problem solved.

2. A PLAIN PLANE ERROR

As I mentioned before I worked for Southern Airways. Our airline was unique with a special smiley face painted on the nose of each airplane, saying, "Have a Nice Day."

During my first week as a flight attendant many years ago, I worked hard to remember and follow all the regulations we had learned in training. Of course, the pilots and other attendants spotted us a mile away in our "temporary" uniforms. The majority of co-workers were helpful, knowing we were "green" and had a lot to learn about our jobs.

On my first trip, we were on a 75-passenger jet headed from Memphis to Chicago. We acted as if we knew the ropes like the seasoned attendants. As I was walking down the aisle, a passenger stopped me.

"Excuse me, ma'am, how long have you been flying?" he asked.

I casually glanced at my watch, and said, "Oh, about 15 minutes."

His face turned pale as if the plane would start to go down since I was new on the job.

This one particular trip we were on the old Martin 404 prop plane with a capacity of 40 passengers. I was the only flight attendant, so I had a lot of duties. A veteran pilot assigned me a new duty.

He said, "Every time before take-off, go in the back, and push a particular button; don't forget, it is very important for the flight."

"Yes sir," I replied. I was already intimidated by this captain, and I was trying my best to do everything perfectly.

Before every take-off, I ran to push the button, as instructed. Then, I got so busy, I forgot all about the button. I was reluctant to confess my omission to the pilot, but I knew I had to tell him. Timidly, I knocked on the cockpit door.

When I told the Captain about my error, he started laughing and said, "Well, don't worry about it; I was playing a joke on you. That button flushes the toilet."

Chapter 8

SMALL TOWNS

1. FREAKY

My first teaching job was in Jackson, Georgia, and I commuted from Barnesville to Jackson every day. The crazy thing was my assignment. I was hired to teach kindergarten, and my college degree was in high school English and Spanish. I really needed the job. The class had over 30 children with one assistant. There were no desks and very little supplies. Boy, was I in for a giant challenge!

One afternoon, I was driving home and got behind a huge MACK truck. I could not see anything in front of him, or on either side. Suddenly, I heard a gigantic ripping noise on top of my little white Toyota SR5. I thought "Rodan" had grabbed my leather roof with its enormous claws. ("Rodan" was a giant monster bird in a 1956 Japanese horror movie) Very creepy!

Large and small pieces of leather were swirling around my car and blowing all over the highway. A long telephone wire was flapping in the breeze.

For several minutes, I kept driving in total shock as to what had occurred. No sign of Rodan anywhere. Thank the Lord! Then, I began to put the event together. That monster truck in front of me was flying at top speed. He failed to slow down as he approached a low wire hanging across the road. Possibly, he never saw it, numskull. Anyhow, his truck cab hit the wire, which temporarily attached itself to something, maybe, the windshield wipers. And, the crazy man kept forging ahead. By now, the wire had stretched forward way beyond its capacity; and like an enormous rubber band it snapped back slashing the wire into pieces.

Unfortunately for me, the tremendous force of the wire's backlash screamed over the truck top and struck my car roof. The wire seared my beautiful black vinyl top straight down the middle. That explained the shower of leather pieces falling from the sky, and swirling like a whirlwind around my car and up and down the road. I was relieved that I had not encountered Rodan, but was heartsick about my cute Toyota. I shook my fist at the crazy truck driver as his truck careened on down the highway. He never stopped. I was mad and sad.

Here was the thing: in the 1970s car dealerships did not fix vinyl replacements on cars.

The serviceman said, "I have an idea: we can remove the bits of black leather still stuck to the top, sand it smooth, and cover the damaged roof with paint. What color do you want?"

"Hmm...sounds like the only choice I have. But I like it. How about a splashy bright yellow?"

He scraped, cussed, sanded, cussed and painted the top. A superb job. He was happy. I was thrilled. It was the talk of the town.

2. IS THAT GOD?

In the late 1970s, jobs in teaching and coaching brought us to live in Hancock County, as I mentioned before. Before we moved to the area, we were offered a cabin to rent on Rocker pond, which was several miles from the tiny town of Sparta. To get to the cabin, we drove out Augusta Highway, turned left onto a dirt road and bounced on down the path to its location on the pond.

After the first mile, the Male Academy, a large three-story Southern house, came into view. Abandoned and empty, it presented a scary sight when the moon rose behind it. The light shone through the branches of a dead tree, and strips of torn curtains blew out the open windows. The mailbox was out in front of the academy, so the mailman came no further.

We lived a mile further down the path. I used to say, "We lived so far back in the sticks, even the mailman was scared to go there." Our daughter was about two and a half at the time. I tried to attend as many ball games in support of our school as I could, which meant carrying Ashley with me.

One particular night, Ashley and I drove by ourselves (not the wisest thing to do) to a basketball game a few hours away. It was a cold, rainy night when we began the late trip home. Then, one of the tires blew out on a desolate stretch of road. Of course, this was before cell phones. At first, I thought it was safer to stay in the car with hopes that someone from the school would stop. Then, I tried to jack up the car, but being on a hill, the jack started to give way.

Many cars went by returning from the game, but no one could see who we were through the rain. Then, I began to fear that whoever stopped for us might take advantage of our dire situation. I prayed and promised God if He would help us, I would stop driving late at night. I decided to go to the nearest house for help. It was pitch dark, and I could not see the road. Somehow, in the darkness, I struggled to walk in my boots and carry Ashley as it was raining. I strained to see the white line—on the edge of the slippery road—which was the only thing I could see.

Ashley started crying, and said, "Mama, I am scared."

I was, too, but could not tell her.

"Don't worry; God is going to send someone to help us," I said.

After, maybe half a mile, a man stopped, asking if we needed help.

"We **do** need help, but…I am afraid to go with you," I said.

Then, he explained he was a Mr. Calloway connected with our school and named some of the players and students. I breathed a sigh of relief!

Ashley looked at him and asked, "Is that God?"

"No, but he is the next closest thing," I said, "God sent him to help us."

Then, he drove us back to our car, changed our tire, and we drove home. He was definitely our guardian angel, and I knew God was protecting us. I will never forget him and his special kindness on that horrible, dark, scary night. Also, I have kept my promise to God by not driving late at night and not driving alone.

Just Heavenly

Make yourself familiar with the angels, and behold them frequently in spirit; for without being seen, they are present with you.

-St. Francis de Sales

3. THINGS THAT GO BUMP IN THE NIGHT

My husband and I had several encounters with critters when we were living in the cabin on Rocker pond. Several folks in town had already warned us of poisonous snakes, spiders, and rabid animals. Any time we heard a bump or thump during the night, we became nervous.

One night, I heard something moving around in the kitchen cabinet under the sink. We got up and came up with a plan. We got two chairs, flashlights, a frying pan and a broom, our weapons. We stood on the two chairs in front of the cabinet thinking we would be above the critter if or when it came out. Slowly, I opened the cabinet doors and shined the dim beam of the light inside. Immediately, I saw the long, black head of the creature.

"There it is!" I yelled.

Wham! Wham!

We hit it over and over with the frying pan and broom until it fell out onto the floor. It never had a chance. We had "killed" a black pot handle.

He said, "I will tell you one thing…if you ever tell this story to anyone, I'll kill ya."

Shhhhh. Don't mention I said anything.

4. MY PAPA

In the ole days, fishermen used many ways to catch fish. Although some of the methods were deemed illegal, few people got caught if they were out in the country. I was talking about mygranddaddy, "PaPa," and how he fished.

Well, he took this old telephone and let the cable dangle down into the creek. He had some way to crank it that sent out an electric spark. That electric current shocked the fish and they just lay still. Papa got his fishing net, and scooped them right up.

Some times during the year, my daddy told me what else PaPa did. You see, PaPa was a very smart kind of man. He crawled up a tree limb that forked over a slew of

Shoulderbone Creek where he lived. When he saw several fish, he fired his shotgun into the creek. Those shots shocked the fish, too, for a few minutes. Then, he leaned down holding onto the tree limb with one hand and his fishing net in the other. He drew them up.

His "fishing" resulted in some delicious, fried fish for family and friends. During a family reunion, I looked over and saw PaPa's shotgun sitting in the corner. I pointed to the gun and said, "Hey, everybody, there's PaPa's fishing pole."

(from Chase Lovejoy)

5. AIN'T NOTHING BUT A HOUND DOG

The owners' son had an old hound dog down there who immediately "took up" with us. His name was Bill. Something was not quite right about ole Bill, but he loved me. He never missed an opportunity to sneeze on me, which apparently was his idea of affection. Being his "sneezee," I now experienced the feeling of being a Kleenex.

One day, I asked Mr. Rocker, "What actually happened to Bill that made him, shall I say, 'different'?"

Mr. Rocker replied, "One day he was chasing a car down the highway. Suddenly, a telephone pole stepped in front of him, and...*Wham!*"

"Oh, no!" I exclaimed.

"Yep, old Bill has never been the same, and neither has the telephone pole."

I shook my head, "Oh, how terrible."

When we moved to Milledgeville, Mr. Rocker said, "You know, Bill has to go with you."

"Oh, yes, we love ole Bill."

By then, he had learned another display of his deep devotion besides sneezing. If we were on the steps, he put his arm (I mean, his leg) around my shoulder. He sat as close as possible to me. You could say, we had really bonded. And, by "bonded," I mean Bill was glued to my side, like Velcro. He loved me as much as I loved him.

After we settled into our new neighborhood, I noticed folks always stared at Bill and me. Immediately, I sensed their jealousy of our close relationship. They put on sunglasses so we could not tell exactly which direction they were looking. But, I was not easily fooled; I knew the truth. Once in a while, they pointed our way and covered their mouths to hide their slight grins. They snickered, and whispered snide comments to each other. It was impossible for them to hide their envy.

"Hey, Buddy, what kind of weird scarf is she wearing?" one guy asked.

"Man, that ain't no scarf; that is her dog Bill draped around her shoulder."

"What? That is one funny ole hound dog."

"Well, what do you expect with a dog named Bill?"

Chapter 9
ADVENTURES IN MILLEDGEVILLE

1. THE BREAK-IN

Years ago, as a single parent raising two children, my piggy bank ran low most of the time. We scraped by, and I had even gotten a hand-me-down refrigerator from my aunt. I believed I lived in a safe neighborhood, but one day I came home and heard someone breathing heavily and gasping to catch his breath. My first thought: An intruder had come in and dashed quickly to hide when he heard me.

My heart was wildly thumping as I dialed my neighbor.

"Hey Rob, can you come over? I think someone has broken in."

"Sure," he said.

Within 60 seconds, Rob was at my door; he was a runner. He came in and paused to hear the steady, wheezing noise. While I stood silently and pointed toward the pantry door, he walked over and yanked it open. Whew! No one there. Of course, in my panicky state, I had no plan of action if we actually **did** find someone hiding.

As the breathing continued, we searched my small kitchen, which only had a tiny pantry and doors to the laundry area. As we tiptoed around my living room looking under furniture and behind curtains, we agreed that somehow the sound was coming from the kitchen area.

Rob put his ear to the refrigerator and said, "Guess what? The raspy breathing is coming from your refrigerator."

"What?" I was surprised and embarrassed. We vowed to never tell another living soul.

Later, my friend Janet joked, "You don't need to worry about your refrigerator as long as it is breathing; but if it stops, it's a goner."

Of course, my repair man (who I had on speed dial) returned to work on my "over-rated icebox." As he left, he patted the refrigerator, and said, "Sorry, I've done all I can do," as if he were a doctor finishing up a surgery.

Sure enough, about six months later my refrigerator sputtered a few times and drew its last breath; this time, it was a real goner and departed for appliance heaven.

2. SAD NEWS

Mrs. Mills' beloved husband had died. A few weeks later, some friends called and wanted her to come for a visit. Finally, she decided taking a trip might be the best thing for her. Then, another tragedy occurred: her precious dog died while she was away. Her neighbors were taking care of it.

After her return, she attended a social gathering in her neighborhood. A lady came up to her, "Oh, I was so upset to hear about your loss." The dear lady was referring to Mr. Mills, her husband.

Thinking about her dear pet, Mrs. Mills replied, "Yes, it was very sad. He got sick and crawled up under the house. My wonderful neighbors next door saw him, pulled him out, and buried him in the back yard."

The lady turned pale and fainted.

3. WELL, I'LL BE SCAMMED

There is nothing new about scam artists trying to trick people out of their money or goods. Back in the 1980s I was working at a local bank in Milledgeville, Georgia. We heard about an elderly couple being robbed by a scam artist. He convinced them to give him $250 in cash. He promised them he could invest their money and make them even more cash. Of course, the rascal left with their money, and they never saw him again.

A lady came into the bank and began to relate to me the unfortunate incident. She vowed and declared that she understood what had happened to the couple.

"Honey, the man put a spell on them; they were helpless."

"Oh, how does he do that?" I inquired.

"Listen to me carefully, now. I know exactly how he did it."

"You do?"

"When he gets near you, you are overcome by his mystical scent," she whispered.

"Are you kidding?"

"No. That scent overpowers you. You are completely helpless and cannot control what you do."

"Gosh, I have never heard of anything like that," I said.

"Honey, I will tell you. That man could not 'skim-skam' or 'flim-flam' me. I know his secret, and I would hold my nose. That's it, I'm telling you. No way, he could overpower me."

"Honey, I know what my grandma said, 'That scent will get you.'"

"Yes, ma'am, I am sure he could not fool you," I said. "I am glad you solved the mystery and told me about it. I think he would have fooled me," I replied.

The lady believed the "power of scent" with all her heart and soul. I was almost convinced myself. After that, the main problem for me was how everyone stared when I wore a clothespin on my nose. (We did not have those cool little masks back then.) The worse part was the darn clothespin pinched like crazy and left a dent on my nose.

4. THINGS ARE NOT ALWAYS WHAT THEY SEEM

In Milledgeville, I played for a women's softball league. Often my five-year-old daughter went with me to the games. She loved eating a hamburger or hotdog at the concessions stand for supper. Then we had a deal about her getting something sweet. She had to behave in the stands during the game, and her reward was candy, ice cream, or whatever she wanted.

One particular night, she was really impatient for her treat. Every inning or so, she called me to the fence, "Mama, can I have my treat now?"

"No, not yet, you have to wait a while."

A few minutes later, she would be at the fence again. About the fifth inning, my team was at bat. I was on third base, ready to score. Our batter hit a hard line drive down the third base line. Just as I whipped my head around to run home, the ball hit me squarely on the forehead. Gosh, this story sounds very familiar. Everything went dark; I was out cold.

When I regained consciousness, players were gazing down at me. Someone had put a cold cloth on my head. Then, a little face moved very close to mine. It was Ashley.

"Mama, can I have my snow cone now?" she whispered.

"Sure," I mumbled groggily.

She shot off like she was blown from a cannon! Straight to the concession stand with her money to buy a snow cone. (Someone later told me.)

Meanwhile, my team members who had not heard her question, kept saying, "Oh, she was so sweet to come out and see about you."

"She is adorable."

"I don't know if my child would come out or not."

5. FURRY

When Ashley was around four or five years old, she saw someone's wig lying on the bed. The way the brown hair curled around, she thought it was a dog. She pointed at it, and asked, "Dog?" We were having a family get together, so we called in every sister, cousin, aunt, or whoever was in the house at that time for her repeat performance. Everyone howled with laughter every time she did it.

About a week later, my friend and I took our kids out to a restaurant. The minute our waitress appeared, Ashley pointed to her wig, and said, "Dog?"

"She is so cute. What did she say?" the waitress asked.

"Oh, I don't know," I replied.

Meanwhile Ashley continued to point and say "dog."

I looked at the waitress and said, "Oh, I can't understand her half the time." How could I politely tell the waitress that either she looked like a dog, or her hair did?

6. BLOW YOUR OWN HORN

A beautiful, sophisticated lady was driving her Chrysler New Yorker down the road. When she stopped at a traffic light, her car engine died. She continually turned the ignition key on and off, but nothing happened.

Meanwhile, a man drove up behind her, and slowed to a complete stop. As they both sat through the changing of lights, he became impatient. Soon his demeanor changed to anger. She was as frustrated as he was but remained calm. She turned various solutions over in her mind.

By now he started honking his horn with his face contorted in a mean grimace. He gripped the steering wheel tightly and continued honking his horn. He was furious!

She reached into her pocketbook, searched for her lipstick and dabbed on a little. Slowly she opened her car door and daintily stepped onto the pavement. Dressed to the nines in her gorgeous silk dress and stilettos, she walked erectly with an air of elegance.

As she approached his car, she tapped gently on his car window.

After lowering the glass, she politely offered, "Hello, sir, I have a great idea. If you could get into my car and attempt to start the engine, I will get into your car and blow the horn. That way, we will both be happy."

(from a family friend)

7. USE IT OR LOSE IT

My parents were always resourceful. Because of hard times, they knew how to take something we had and stretch it a long way. Daddy saw broken-down wagons in the fields along his mail route.

"Mr. Smith, can I buy the wheels on your wagons?"

"No, but you can have them for free."

Daddy took out the wooden hub, cleaned and varnished it. Then, he inserted electrical wires, and lamp parts. He sold the lamps for $25 each, which was a good sale for him. He was an entrepreneur.

Every spring, Daddy sprayed Mama's scuffed-up wooden pocketbooks with a fresh coat of paint and varnish. Good as new.

Luckily, I adhered to the family tradition to make ends meet. As a single parent with two children and living on a shoe string, I knew how to conserve and be resourceful. Along the roadside, I stopped to pick up any wood I could use in my fireplace. I rarely bought wood.

One day at work, I noticed a lot of limbs had fallen into a parking space. Bingo, my lucky day! Quickly I gathered them up and put them in my trunk!

Later that day, my friend Jenny called, "Hey, did you pick up some limbs along the street?"

"Yeah, but how did you know it was me?"

"Look, I'm your friend, and I know you are always looking for wood or something you can use."

"Okay, but what's the problem?" I asked.

"A friend of ours was waiting for the insurance company to see the limbs that damaged her car. Then, she noticed that most of the evidence had disappeared."

"Did you tell her I was a scavenger?"

"No, she already knew."

"Oh, okay. But tell her I have to be resourceful. Sorry, I will go and put all of the limbs back."

Well, you cannot imagine the looks people gave me when I tossed all the wood out of my car back into the parking space. Then, I had to scatter them around to look as if they had fallen naturally. Onlookers continued to stare. You see, being a scavenger can have some embarrassing moments.

After the insurance man's photo shoot, again I returned to the scene of the tree's crime and reloaded the limbs. But, stop. The story does not end there.

Later that day, I put my Styrofoam container of leftover vegetables on the back seat. By eating half of my lunch and saving the rest for supper, I saved money and calories. After work, I walked to my car, and immediately noticed something strange on my food container: two large, skinny insects, about five inches tall, which resembled giant mosquitoes on steroids. Their needle-like suckers were stuck into my container of food. Yuck! It was very creepy.

Apparently, they had been living in or on my scavenged wood, and they came out to dine.

Morals of the story: For future wood pickups, borrow a truck. Never leave food alone in my car. Good eats and sweet treats are allowed in the car only when I am devouring them myself.

8. NITTY GRITTY

Years ago, when I started working in my yard, I began to battle one particular nuisance...no, not my neighbors...ants. Of course, everyone had a perfect remedy; someone mentioned the best Southern pesticide was grits. The next day, I poured an abundant amount of grits (minus the salt and butter) on each mound. Those eager little ants scurried to get some. I hope they took a little bowl back into their mound to share with their Queen. Well, you won't believe this! When I checked on them again, those clever grown-up ants, baby ants, and Queen had packed up their duds overnight and moved. No one said they were nomadic.

Anyway, I continued my sure fire "rid an ant" potion for a while. It did not bother or exterminate them. I am proud to say that one thing happened: the grits affected the culture of the ant society. They started wearing overalls and speaking with a Southern drawl. The last time I saw the Queen, she was wearing a blue jean skirt, boots, and a cowgirl hat. You see, I made a difference!

9. YUMMY

During the 1990s, I worked at the Georgia College library. (Later, I discovered that four out of five aunts also worked there when they attended college.) Our director agreed to our celebration of birthdays. Some scroogey departments did not deem them necessary. With about 25 employees, we were constantly having parties, every few weeks. From the very beginning, no one ever wanted to cut the cake. Finally, I said I would do it and acted like I knew what I was doing. That is how I became the official cake cutter.

When a birthday approached, we sent out emails to let the group know whose birthday it was, time of party, etc. Our computer guy was always late.

One day, when he arrived, I asked "Do you want a piece of cake?"

"Sure." He loved it because I usually cut a big, thick slice for him. I liked him and sympathized with his demanding workload.

When he was almost finished, I said, "Oh, I forgot to mention, I licked the knife a few times; hope you don't mind."

The look on his face...priceless! Of course, I was kidding him, but he was never quite sure. However, he continued to eat the cake every time anyway.

10. HELP! I NEED SOMEBODY

During that time in the library, computers had just come on the scene, and everyone was struggling to learn how to use them. The computer systems had glitches that made the process even more aggravating and difficult. The staff went to workshops to learn how to use them. Of course, within five minutes, my computer screen froze, which was very common then. I was stuck; I could not do anything as the rest of the class was following along. So, I did not learn much from the beginning.

The faculty was much more adept at using computers. They took turns at the "Help Desk" to assist our library patrons (customers). The patrons were trying hard to catch on to computer lingo and learn special keys to do specific things. We were all struggling with the same issues as our patrons.

One day, a lady kept pressing the "Help" key on her computer board and grimacing at the faculty lady at the desk. Finally, she became so frustrated that she stomped up to the Help Desk.

"Ma'am, why won't you help me?"

"Excuse me, what do you mean?" asked the faculty member.

"I keep pressing 'Help,' and you just ignore me."

"Oh, let me explain please. That button does not send me a message."

"Is it broken?" asked the lady.

"No, no. What I mean is the computer 'help' button gives you certain steps to take. It instructs you with specific details to reach the next place you want to go."

"Well, it is definitely NOT doing a very good job," the lady growled. She threw up her arms, and stomped away in disgust.

The faculty lady gave the patron a few minutes to cool off. Then, she walked over to the table where the lady was declaring war on her computer. Such was a typical day in the computer world…for our patrons as well as for ourselves. We were as lost as our patrons because the new technology was dropped on us with very little warning or preparation.

11. PEEPING TOM

An older couple had problems with a Peeping Tom. You know, a guy who looks through windows and watches people. Most people are not particularly thrilled with this behavior. The wife saw a man's head pop up at the window at night and look in at her. She was scared to death. And outraged with the strange man.

One night, she saw him and yelled to her husband, "He's out there, he's out there. Do something."

The husband grabbed his gun and headed outside.

After a few minutes, he returned, "I lost him in the darkness."

"Well, next time I will call the police."

This scenario continued on and off for several weeks. Of course, the husband had no intention of shooting the fellow but thought it satisfied his wife.

Finally, the wife called the police, "Hurry, hurry, we have a Peeping Tom."

"Ma'am, calm down, and explain this Tom that peeps." The policeman was from another country and did not understand the expression. Another policeman grabbed the phone and listened to the lady.

Within five minutes the police arrived, but the man was gone.

Eventually, the husband got sick and tired of the situation.

He told his wife, "I have an idea. Maybe, if you stick your face in the window, it will scare the Peeping Tom away."

The last thing we heard the husband was still suffering with a horrible black eye.

(from my friend at the library)

12. DILEMMA

A college girl had applied for a job at a Mexican restaurant. She was excited about making extra money. When she applied, the manager told her about certain tasks and requirements. She had to buy white blouses and dark skirts, work certain times, and drive 30 miles to Macon to get a form from the Main Office.

She complained to her roommate, "First, I have to spend money on clothes, that I won't wear outside of work, and before I start work, I have to spend money for gas to go out of town. Plus, the time it takes. I don't know if the job is worth it or not."

"Hmm, maybe, I can help," said her roomie.

"What kind of form do you need?"

"It is a WD40, or something like that."

(from a relative)

13. SAY CHEESE

When my daughter Ashley reached her senior year in high school, one of her most anticipated events was the senior cruise. She saved all her baby sitting, birthday, and Christmas money to make all the payments for the trip. She and her friends shopped for "glitzy dresses" to take for the more formal occasions on board.

On the night of the Captain's Dinner they put on their sparkly dresses and heels and arrived dripping with jewelry, and their faces glowing with tons of make-up and lipstick. Giggling and yakking excitedly, this gaggle of friends were having a blast snapping pictures of each other and everyone. Everyone still used cameras then.

During the midst of this photo frenzy, Ashley turned and asked a crew member if he could take a few pictures. Somewhat taken aback, he angled her camera and took several pictures.

Afterwards, one of her friends whispered, "Ash, I can't believe you asked him to take our picture."

"Why, who is he?"

"Oh, he is **just** the **Captain** of the ship," her friend related.

(from a relative)

14. BIRD TWEETS

Okay, people, here is a true bird story I simply have to share. Oh, brother, this author is truly obsessed...

Another thing I tried was directing bluebirds to the birdhouse. When I saw a bluebird in the front yard, I yelled and pointed toward the back yard. Dumb bird was clueless. Then, I tried waving my arms in a forward motion to send them in the right direction where the bluebird house was located. Next, I jumped up and down and waved to get its attention. The bluebird refused to obey my signals and continued on its merry way.

However, in the process I got the attention of the people next door. I caught a glimpse of their miniblinds move up slightly every now and then. I got the biggest kick out of entertaining them.

"Pete, what in the heck are you doing?" nagged Madge.

"Oh, just watching the lady next door," answered Pete.

"Would you help with the groceries, Mr. Snoop? **If** you have time?"

Then, a while later, another bird became **too** attracted to me! As I headed out the door one morning, a bird swooped down very close to my head. I admit I have had some doozy hair-styles, but apparently this one resembled a bird's nest. It was strange. Whenever the children went outside, the swooping bird stayed in the tree. The very second I stepped out the door, the feathered dive bomber zeroed in on my head. No one else. It was only attracted to or obsessed with **me**. Even though I flailed my arms around to scare off the crazed fowl, its antics persisted all afternoon. I could not frighten it away, and I could not go to my car.

I have never believed in reincarnation…that a person could return to Earth…in the form of a bird, or anything else. But this bird actually resembled a teacher who disliked me in the early grades. Of course, I noticed the neighbors' window blind go up for a second and quickly back down. I figured they were watching the bird and us.

"Hey, Pete, quit poking your nose through the blinds."

"But, Madge, that zany bird is back with a vengeance. And, it looks familiar."

"For Pete's sake, Pete, don't act surprised; something is usually happening over there. Mostly, on the crazy side."

"Yes, dear, a little crazy, but more entertaining than you," Pete whispered.

"Huh…What did you say?"

"Oh," I said, "Come in here, I have a great view."

"Let me look," Madge said. "Well, my goodness. That bird does look like the one that attacked Uncle Moe's dusty toupee."

Eventually, the bird went home to its nest to check on its family and finish the latest rerun of *The Birds* by Alfred Hitchcock. Luckily for me, my head was spared.

But don't worry, I have more Bird Tweets. Are you kidding me? We are fed up with these bird scenarios.

Chapter 10
KIDS SAY IT BEST

1. DIRTY BUSINESS

A small boy was talking with the minister. He looked up and asked, "Mr. Preacher, is it true that we are made from dirt?"

"Son, that is true. According to the Bible, "from dust you come and to dust you shall return."

"In that case, you better come to my house."

"Why is that?" asked the minister.

"Cause you need to look under my bed; somebody is either coming or going."

2. HEAVENLY DAZE

My niece Donna asked her mama, "Is Heaven a wonderful place?"

"Oh, yes, it is the most beautiful place you can imagine."

"Why don't we go up there to eat sometime?"

3. WHAT HE HEARD

A pastor overheard children singing, "And the shepherds 'washed their socks' by night." (sic)

"The shepherds watched their flocks by night."

4. EASY ANSWER

Recently, a college friend of mine was talking with her granddaughter. They had just been reading about Adam and Eve in the Garden of Eden. Little Morgan asked, "Mimi, was the Garden of Eden real?"

"Yes, it was a real place."

"Where was it?" asked Morgan.

"Well, no one knows exactly where it was," explained Mimi.

"Why don't they just look it up on the internet?"

5. THE KID IS ALL ABOUT FOOD

Once at a basketball game, Ashley asked me, "Mama, do you have some money for the concession stand?"

"No, I don't think so."

A few minutes later, someone came from the concessions area, "I just wanted you to know that Ashley is down here with your checkbook wanting to buy something."

That little girl of ours knew how things worked, at an early age.

6. TIE BREAKER

When my daughter and son were growing up, they played various board and card games. My daughter Ashley (nicknamed Ash) was about seven years older than my son Tyler (nicknamed Ty).

One day after playing several card games, I heard Ashley say, "Okay, this game is going to be the 'tie' breaker." "

All right," Ty answered in a very irritated tone. "But, **next time**, it is going to be an '**Ash**' breaker."

7. TY AND THE YELLOW JACKETS

I took my kids to Burger King to eat supper. Within a few minutes, they had scarfed down their burger, fries, and drink. Their main thing was to go to the playground as soon as possible.

They headed out to play. Within five minutes, they were back inside.

"What happened?" I asked. "Y'all did not play very long."

"Mama, those flies wearing yellow jackets came out; we were afraid they would sting us," my son related.

8. CAN T FOOL HIM

As the little boy was leaving the airport, he was looking at all the planes. He spotted a big hangar, and said, "Dad, that's where the man who owns the airport lives."

9. SMART MOM

A family was shopping at a Walmart. The children wanted to play on the blood pressure machine, but the mother said, "No children are allowed on that machine."

One of her sons asked, "Mama, where does it say that?"

"Everywhere, honey, everywhere."

10. CAUTION: STRANGE MAN WITH BEARD

When Tyler was small, I never allowed him to eat hard candy. He had gotten choked on a piece once. I was afraid he might choke again.

One Christmas Eve, we drove to the amazing house decorated with hundreds of lights, sets of little lighted houses, deer, sleighs, elves and everything imaginable. The family decorated it yearly especially for all the children in our neighborhood. The lights could be seen from miles away, and people drove long distances to see it. It was a Christmas tradition for the family who started it. They had many storage sheds in the back yard to store all the items during the rest of the year. They started in October taking everything out to test the lights, and get the scenes arranged and organized. A two-month undertaking that they loved.

Once, we were invited inside. You would not believe the hundreds of dolls and more Christmas trees than anyone has ever seen. Usually, on Christmas Eve, Santa stood in front of the house handing out candy. We joined the line of cars to stop and greet him. Finally, we approached the strange man with the beard. Tyler was very wary of him and unsure of getting too close. I coaxed him to roll down the car window.

Tyler shrunk back as Santa shook his hand and bellowed, "HO, HO, HO !"

"Let's go, Mama," Tyler said. Just as I started moving, Santa slipped him a piece of candy.

As we drove away, Tyler unwrapped the candy….it was HARD. Oh, great.

Immediately, if not sooner, he yelled at the top of his lungs, "Santa is trying to kill me, Santa is trying to kill me."

Innocent Santa had no idea he was a murderer.

11. HOOD IN OUR HOOD

My kids and I were living in a great neighborhood. Families with children lived up and down the whole street. They always had someone to play with, and we felt they were safe. Then, I noticed an older guy in our 'hood. He was a motorcycle dude, dressed in leather, chains, and covered in tattoos. This was in the 1980s, and we never saw or met many guys like him, then. Normally, the only tattoos we ever saw were on military guys. We were a bit wary of him (needless to say).

The kids absolutely thought he was the coolest guy ever. He began to fix their bicycles, so we became more accustomed to his being around.

One day, I stopped down at the bottom of the street where all the boys had encircled him as he worked on a bike. All of a sudden, he grabbed a boy's long hair, reached in his pocket, and snatched out a switchblade. I held my breath. What was he doing?

He clicked the blade—and out popped a comb that he ran through the boy's hair. We all laughed.

Well, as soon as we started breathing again. I am sure the whole scene was intended as a joke to catch me off guard. Well, it worked.

12. HALEY, OUR GRANDDAUGHTER

Her first camp meeting, Haley was five years old when she attended her first camp meeting with our family. If she wanted someone to pick her up, she said, "Hug me up." After a night service, all the kids raced down to the store at the old hotel. She surveyed all the candy bars, ice cream, and drinks for a few minutes. Then, she piped up, "No healthy food here."

During the sermon, I always supplied her with a little notebook to draw in. She was very intent on her drawing, but those little ears were totally tuned in to what the preacher was saying. I was surprised when she made comments about his sermon. He said to enter the kingdom of heaven, you had to be born again.

"Mimi, born again? How can you be born again?"

"By accepting Christ."

"I just don't know how you can really be born again," she said.

Next the preacher said, "Saul was a man who changed."

Haley asked, "Mimi, how can a man change?"

"God can change a man's heart when he believes in Jesus," I said.

"Oh," she said.

13. FISHING ETIQUETTE WITH HALEY

Really? Is this another fishing episode? This writer is totally obsessed with these slimy fishie thingies. Seriously, I do not think I can take another one. (She will never know if I completely skip this part, right?)

As with any sport, there are usually rules of etiquette to follow. Two rules come to mind: Be quiet. Do not let the tip of the pole touch the water. So, here it goes. I am teaching my granddaughter Haley to fish at the age of five. I am trying my doggone best to stir up her interest in fishing. We are down at our creek in the springtime.

"Okay, you have to be very quiet," I whispered.

"Why?"

"You will scare the fish away."

"Oh, okay," she said.

"Do not let your cane pole touch the water."

"Why?"

"My daddy always said that frightened the fish, too. You will get used to being quiet and walking softly," I explained. Unlike myself, when I catch one, I start jumping up and down.

"Look, look, everybody!" I get hyper-excited.

Next, I kick over my can of worms and trip over my cane pole, breaking it in half. Yes, I know; I should remain calm. Haley is trying her best to teach me how to be quiet. In a little while Popoo, Haley's name for my husband, comes roaring up on his four-wheeler.

"Haley, do you want to ride?"

"Yes sir," she exclaims as her eyes brighten.

Off they fly! So much for fishing time!

14. BABY QUAKE

Haley was staying with us, and I was reading her a bedtime story. It was April 6, 2017. We had bad thunderstorms on and off that night. About 9:30, we felt a big shake and our windows rattled.

"Haley, did you feel and hear that?"

"I did, what was it?"

"I think lightning hit something."

The next morning, we heard that it was a 2.5 earthquake, about three miles southwest of Sparta. Possibly four to five miles from our house. My granddaughter and I shared our one and only shake and quake together. (It was a big deal since we rarely have earthquakes in Georgia)

Chapter 11

WHO IS CONFUSED?

1. PUT THE CAT OUT

My husband's grandmother, Ma-Ma was in the nursing home in her later years. At her home, she always had a cat, but no animals were allowed in her present facility. Whenever we visited her, her roommate, Alice was present. As time passed, both of them became more confused. Once my cousin Sandra visited her.

Ma-Ma said, "Sandra, put that cat out."

"Ma-Ma, there is not a cat in here."

Their chit chat continued while Alice was the silent observer.

Again, Ma-Ma said, "Can you put that cat out?"

"I told you; there is no cat in here."

Finally, on the third request, Sandra rolled up a towel (to resemble a cat), gently picked it up, and tossed it out the door.

Alice said, "Sandra, I have been worried about her, but now, I am worried about you."

2. WHO AM I?

Later on, Ma-Ma and Alice were in their room talking. Ma-Ma sensed from their conversation, that Alice's mind might be slipping. Finally, Ma-Ma said, "Alice, do you know my name?"

Alice blinked her eyes and stared at Ma-Ma without saying a word.

Then, she said, "You can walk right down there to that desk, and they can tell you."

3. CAR IN A BOX

Many years ago, my brother lived in a house on a steep hill. He came home from work as usual and parked his beloved sports car on the hilltop next to his house. It was already dark, so he could not see the caution tape at the bottom of the hill. Meanwhile, the DOT (Department of Transportation) had worked on a water main next to his driveway. They had not finished their work, and covered a large hole with a tarpaulin.

The next morning, Leon came out, cranked his car, and went back inside. A few minutes later, he walked out carrying his coffee mug and briefcase.

Whoa, something was missing. He started looking around thinking, *This must be a joke...where is my car?* Then, he gazed downward. His beloved Mercedes had rolled down the driveway, made a precise turn at the rectangular hole, and parked itself perfectly...in the hole.

His sports car was way ahead of its time. It was the first driverless car with perfect parking skills if you wish to park underground. Unbelievable! An exact fit.

Knowing my brother, I am sure he said some very choice words about his car AND the hole. Words he had not learned in Sunday School. He called the wrecker service to hoist it out; it was a tedious job for them, too. They had to carefully hoist it upward without denting the sides, top or anything. Bystanders heard a few choice words from them, too. Luckily, the men did not leave any scratches or "Dents in my brother's Mercedes Benz."

4. HEN PECKED

My sister had a fingernail on one finger that curved downward. For some reason, I thought she said, "I put my finger in a chicken pen when I was little, and a hen pecked the tip of my fingernail. After that, the nail curved down."

When I mentioned it to her, she said, "No, I did not get hen pecked."

Her husband Don immediately said, "Actually she saved that for me."

Chapter 12
A SHRINK IN TIME

1. FOOT IN MOUTH

Psychiatrist speaking to his nurse: "When you answer the phone, would you please say we are very busy? Don't keep saying it's a mad house."

(from a sign in psychiatrist office in Macon, May 12, 2014)

2. MISSING MARBLES

Recently, I had an appointment with my psychiatrist. (I was diagnosed with bipolar disorder over 20 years ago.) As we were talking, he remembered he had several marbles in his pocket. He explained that his granddaughter was coming by the office, and he always gave her different colored marbles. Then, he stood up, reached into his pocket and continued, "Excuse me, one minute, I was checking my pocket to make sure I still had all of my marbles."

Then, realizing another meaning of what he said, we both laughed.

"I totally understand."

"You know, it is not good for a psychiatrist to be missing some of his marbles."

I agreed. (I love my psychiatrist: we can joke about almost everything.)

3. DOC IS IN

My brother-in-law and I were talking. He said, "If I went to a psychiatrist, here is what I would say...

> **Don:** "I have a particular problem with my wife."
> **Psychiatrist:** "What is it?"
> **Don:** "You could say she rules me like a dictator."
> **Psychiatrist:** "Well, exactly, how does that work?"
> **Don:** "She tells ME what MY opinion is going to be."
> (from Don Cardell)

Chapter 13

THE GREAT OUTDOORS

1. GOOD OLE CANE POLE FISHING

(Oh, great, here we go again with these tiresome fishing things.)

Questions we ponder:

1. Why do fish bite your friend's line and not yours, 18 inches away?
   - Your friend's worms have a worse smell.
   - He spits on his bait.
   - The fish have a personal grudge against you.
   - It is one of life's mysteries.

2. What makes fish suddenly stop biting?
   - Time for them to go to "school."
   - They are trying to diet.
   - They have to go check Facebook.

3. How do fish outsmart us?
   - They are in cahoots with stumps, sunken limbs, and vines which get you tangled.

- They love to laugh when a tree branch snags your rig and displays it like a string of Christmas lights.
- They nibble just a little at the time until all of your bait is gone. They know that you are waiting for the cork to go under completely (which may mean it is a larger fish).
- Their favorite is the "spy fish watch"...as you look away for a split second, the spy fish signals the biter fish who grabs your line, ties it around a root and gobbles up your worms, or crickets. (This is the oldest trick in the book.)

3. Ten Things a Fisherman or Fisherlady Will Never Say
   - The fish that broke my line was only about five inches long.
   - There is no such thing as a lucky fishing pole.
   - Sure, I will tell you my secret fishing spots.
   - Hey, everybody come over here...they are really biting.
   - My spouse called; I have to go home to keep the kids.
   - I hate that pond because the fish are always too big.
   - I can't bait my own hook because the worms are too slimy.
   - I stopped fishing because I got so tired of reeling in all those fish.
   - A fisherman never lies.
   - Yes, sir, Mister Game Warden, I caught four fish over the limit and kept them.

Chapter 14
LIFE OF A RECRUITER

1. OVERHEARD CONVERSATIONS

My life as an admissions recruiter for Georgia College in Milledgeville began in 1999. I had to get used to eating alone in restaurants. I was self-conscious at first, so normally, I carried a newspaper or magazine with me. Usually, however, I found myself listening to people's conversations.

Once when I was waiting on my order at a Huddle House, I caught the conversation of two couples in the booth next to me. One couple was talking about their night's stay at a hotel (obviously not a five-star place). The lady said, "That hotel was so cheap we had to return our toothbrushes the next morning." Hopefully, she was kidding.

Another time, I was eating at a wonderful restaurant and was seated near a very talkative group of people. One man was talking, and his voice trailed off as a tall, beautiful, slender girl walked past. She was wearing a dress composed of minimal material (low cut on the top, too short on the bottom, and too tight everywhere else.) Everyone stared at her...especially the men. And, they clammed up.

Finally, the man who had been talking, caught his breath, and looked back at the people at his table, "Wow, I've seen more cotton in the top of a medicine bottle than in her dress." The rest of the men were still in a trance, and just shook their heads up and down.

2. I M ON THE ROAD AGAIN

Traveling with my job was a totally new experience, and I was very excited about all the new adventures that awaited. My mission was to meet high school students around the state and convince them to start their college career with us.

At one of the schools, the students stopped at my table to ask questions:

"Do you have change for a dollar?"

"Are you the school nurse?"

"Why are you here?"

They did not see all my banners, and brochures advertising my college.

At college fairs many colleges meet at one high school, on the same day, with all their brochures, applications, handouts, and novelty pens to dazzle potential students.

Once, another recruiter standing next to me kept peeking under her table. I noticed her behavior, but did not say a word. Then, she said, "Please don't tell anyone but I brought my new pet with me."

"Your secret is safe with me," I said.

"It is the cutest little Vietnamese pot-bellied pig ever," she continued.

"Oh, okay."

"It was new so I could not leave it at home during this college fair."

"Yeah, I guess not."

She continued peeking underneath the table, petting the pig, and talking sweetly to it.

Finally, she left early with little "Bubbles," and I never saw her again.

3. MORE OVERNIGHTS

I stayed overnight in motels, met other interesting characters at Waffle Houses, and learned about life on the road. Normally, we stayed in certain motels, and most of them were nice. One exception was the one in Griffin, Georgia. What I learned there:

Don't stay in hotels located close to busy highways. The noise from the 18-wheelers zooming up and down the road all night almost knocked me out of bed.

When the drivers leaned out of their truck windows to toss their cigarettes butts, and cans, everything hit my door. That is what I mean by close.

And, if the room rate is cheaper than usual, beware! The extras you get, may not be what you want. Mine included two flying cockroaches.

When I told the front desk lady, "Cockroaches? Are you kidding?" she gasped.

"No, ma'am, I know it is extremely hard to believe they reside in your ultra-pristine motel."

"It certainly is," she said.

"Do you have any insect spray, by any chance?"

"No, we don't. We don't ever need it."

Yeah, right, and people lost in the desert never need water.

Once my supervisor's extra included a lizard sitting on the clock that leapt onto his bed unexpectedly, when he was in it. One thing about it: Always a new adventure or story to tell.

4. SIGNS

Often when I have traveled, I constantly was looking for signs and asking for directions to towns or schools. I realized a lot of people have no idea where they **are**, and certainly cannot help you get somewhere else.

Once in a quickie store, I asked for directions to a school. The cashier was completely clueless about her surroundings. She sent me all around the country-side, through the mountains on an hour-long trip and back to the same quickie store where I began.

The school was only a few miles from her location.

Oh, well. One thing about getting lost is that you do get to see sights you haven't seen before.

In 2000, I saw a sign up in Summerville, Georgia, the "House of Pain, for Tattoos and Piercings," which made me cringe. The popularity of piercing, or being stuck, stamped and tortured had not hit it big locally yet. (Call me weird, but I am a person who does not adore pain.)

Another sign, in the West End area of Atlanta that same year was rather strange and morbid:

"Best Buy Caskets." First of all, caskets were not on my shopping list, plus one would never fit in my car.

"Roadkill Cafe (You Kill 'Em, We Grill 'Em)." I saw this doozy in Anderson, South Carolina. Are you kidding me? I don't think we will eat there.

On McDonald's playground, "Playground Closed, Sorry Management." When I saw this sign, I laughed; I realized they did not mean to call the Management sorry. They intended to say the owners regretted the inconvenience of the playground being closed.

"Hemlock Street." Oh, my. Many doctors' offices and several hospitals are located on this street in Macon. One of the meanings of hemlock is poison, so it is better not to think about that when I visit my doctor or the hospital there.

5. GOOD OLE TANNIE

Since I was the newest Admission Recruiter (and the oldest), I naturally got the worst van to drive. (I named all the vehicles according to their colors.) My van, Tannie, had several annoying quirks, sort of like myself: an odd interaction between the seat belt and gas lid lever, windshield wiper issues, and the engine running hot.

Other than that, driving "Tannie" was smooth sailing. Our fleet was Goldie, Greenie, Whitie, and Tannie. As I rode down the highway, if I shifted slightly on the seat, the other end of the seat belt snatched the gas tank lever, and the gas lid popped open. Immediately, if not sooner, everybody and their brother honked their horns and pointed toward the gas tank lid. I waved until I could pull off the road to manually close the lid again.

I continued my journey and within five minutes, *Pop!* There goes the lid again.

I realized it was a conspiracy. Honking horns, pointing, and blinking lights continued until I fixed the lid again.

The windshield wipers had issues, too. They had two speeds...on and off. No option to spray soapy water or water on the windshield. No slow, medium, or fast spraying. Just on or off. I guess I have been spoiled by driving cars with accessories that really work.

My supervisor warned me that, at times, ole Tannie ran hot. No problem, I knew what to do. One day, the engine started smoking, and I pulled over to the next gas station. I asked the mechanic for a container of water. I lifted the hood, and saw that someone had scratched a message on the engine, "Pour water here."

I took the advice, and a few seconds later, I felt something splashing on my shoes. Great! Some joke! The water went into the tank and right out another hole that was not supposed to be there. Funny joke…haha! Never a dull moment with "Tannie."

The craziest part was the vehicle maintenance procedures we had to follow while we were out on the road (to disaster). I called the maintenance supervisor.

"Hey, Tony, I am having a problem with the water tank on Tannie."

"What sort of problem?"

"The water tank has a hole in it."

"Of course, it does; that is where you pour in the water."

"No, no, I mean it has an extra hole on the tank bottom."

"How did you do that?" I knew he would think it was my fault.

"Tony, I could fix it myself, but I am low on bubble gum and duct tape."

"Okay, Ms. Smarty, I will get permission for a work order, and call you back in a few hours."

"Did you say hours?"

"Yes."

"No worries, I will slosh around in my shoes and get something to eat if they will let me enter a restaurant like this."

"Sounds good."

Boy, do I love this job!

6. WHAT A PLACE!

Sometimes I had to travel quite a ways to get to my recruiting area. During my visit to Hartwell High School in north Georgia, everyone said "While you are up here, you ought to go by the Jockey Lot; it's not too far from here."

Although I knew I had no interest in becoming a jockey, I went. Wow! I discovered rows and rows of permanent tin buildings, and covered stands, filled with everything from farming equipment to jewelry to hot dogs to artwork and live puppies. The booths were manned (and "womaned") by some interesting characters. One vender was singing away, and said, "You know, I have always wished I could sing." And become famous. The boy working with her said, "Now, **I wish** you could, too…sing, that is."

My kind of place…good stuff and great junk! Honey, you don't <u>need</u> any of it, but the total experience is a blast.

7. A BED AND BREAKFAST, ALMOST

Another time I stayed at a beautiful, historic bed and breakfast (B&B) in Sautee, Georgia. Nestled on a mountainside, the inn showcased an absolutely gorgeous view. I really expected my night to be an interesting one. Usually the host and hostess of B&B's were very congenial and gave a tour of the house. Normally, there were other guests to meet which gave an extra layer of security. Plus, they explained the breakfast arrangements, check-out, and other rules.

When I arrived, a very thin, strange-looking man checked me into the place. No mention of a wife. Something about him gave me an uneasy feeling. He said the only phone was at the desk. Also, because of my early departure time the next morning, I would not get breakfast. I enjoyed a delicious dinner in the dining room and was joined by other people since the restaurant was open to the public. Then, everyone left. There were no other guests staying except the creepy innkeeper and me. Not good! I was not thrilled to be the only boarder, but I was very tired, and there were no other motels for 40 miles. Not to mention, no television, and no phone in my room. This was a long time ago before we had cell phones. I could not call for help even I wanted to.

I was convinced that I had watched too many scary movies. I was a little afraid, but went straight to my room, bolted the door, and did not set foot outside. Unlike the females in those horror flicks, who walked all around, up and down stairs to different floors all night long, I did not want a strange encounter like theirs. They seemed scared and yet felt compelled to go into every room including the attic and basement. Eventually, an alien monster or crazy being snatched them. This beautiful place was nothing like I expected.

I did get the first "B," a bed. And, I hoped to get my other "B," breakfast. But the main thing on my mind was making a Bee line out of the place early the next morning.

Chapter 15
WHAT PEOPLE SAID

1. I WAS FRAMED

I had gone into the picture frame shop and was discussing pictures, borders and such with the frame guy. I was a frequent customer, so he knew me fairly well. He and I were having a good conversation. All of a sudden, he stopped talking, and looked closely at my eyes.

"You know, you can have those bags under your eyes fixed."

"Huh? What did you say?" I uttered.

"The insurance will even pay for you to have the surgery."

Shocked beyond words, I was very insulted, and I mumbled something. Then, I finished my transaction, left the store, never to return.

2. CASHIER

One day I went shopping at wonderful store I loved. I was very excited since I rarely had the opportunity to go there. I could not believe my luck; I found several things that I liked, and they actually fit me. As I was checking out, the cashier said, "Ma'am, if you had come yesterday, everything was one half off."

"Oh, really?" I always enjoy a slap in the face when I am having fun.

"Oh, yes, we had a big sale," she said.

"Well, I am so glad you told me about all the money I could have saved and ruined my day," I uttered. She seemed shocked I said anything, but she did not mind being rude and sassy to me.

3. STICKS AND STONES

On our lunch hour, my girlfriend and I went into our favorite restaurant. They served the best country cooking with a big assortment of meats, vegetables, rolls, and dessert. As we were standing in line, I saw a doctor I knew.

We talked a minute, and he said, "I never noticed you had freckles all over your face."

I was speechless. Again. Normally, my makeup hid all my blemishes and flaws. Or, so I thought. Wow, can you believe what people will say?

Pleasant words are as a honeycomb; sweet to the soul, and health to the bones. (Proverbs 16:24)

4. DON T KICK EM WHEN THEY ARE DOWN

I was talking with a lady at work one day. We were discussing husbands, and I had recently gone through a divorce. I was not feeling the greatest about my situation. Finally, she quoted, "God can bring you a man, but can't make him stay."

"You don't say," I responded. And, I would have been much happier if she had not revealed her depressing quote at that particular time.

"There is no tranquilizer in the world more effective than a few kind words" (Pearl Bailey). I needed a lot of kind words after that one.

5. WE ROCK

In the 1990s, one of our library co-workers at Georgia College, who was single, met a great guy at the University of Georgia library. They had a whirlwind romance, and soon they were engaged. We were thrilled for our dear friends. Being all caught up in the details of the upcoming wedding, we decided to pool our money for the perfect wedding gift for them. (If there is such an animal as that.)

The bride was a very practical person. No fuss, no frills! She was not the least bit interested in china, cookware, or anything couples usually get. We all liked her and were determined to get them something they would use.

Continually we asked her, "What do you and Stephen really want for a wedding gift?"

She hemmed and hawed around, "Okay, what we want are granite stones for the ditch in our back yard." (I said they were practical people.)

Several people headed to "The Stone Store" near Athens to pick out the perfect stones and make delivery arrangements. By the way, wrapping rocks are a real headache.

When the delivery was made, the happy couple called, "We are very happy with our stones—they are perfect."

Later, at the wedding reception, our group was having a good time yakking, laughing, and wolfing down the cake and punch.

We were taken aback at first, when a lady came over to us and asked, "Aren't ya'll the rock group?"

6. NO ONE WAS LISTENING

When we stopped at Key West on a cruise, we took a trolley tour of the town. As we passed the very famous cemetery of 1847 containing over 60,000 souls, the tour guide pointed out graves of unique characters and unusual epitaphs. Gloria M. Russel's tombstone was inscribed with "I'm just resting my eyes." One epitaph on a newer mausoleum says, "I Always Dreamed of Owning a Small Place in Key West." The most popular tombstone belonged to Mrs. B.P. "Pearl" Roberts, a local hypochondriac. During her life, she had 18 operations, mostly on her stomach, but she had trouble convincing her family and friends she was really ill. She complained all the time, and yet, her friends asked, "How can you be sick, you're always smiling?"

Finally, she told her husband she was not long for this world. She picked out her favorite pink dress and said, "No jewelry." She died at the age of 50, and her epitaph read, "I Told You I Was Sick."

7. NEVER WAS HEARD A DISCOURAGING WORD

A student at our local college wanted to be an assistant to the men's basketball team.

"Hey, coach, do you need any help?"

"No, we have a paid assistant we hired a few months ago. I wish we had a position for you."

"All right, coach, then I will see you tomorrow," the guy replied.

The coach was perplexed about the guy's response. Sure enough, the guy showed up the next day at practice. He retrieved basketballs when they went out-of-bounds, and helped out the entire practice.

Afterwards, Coach Sellers, in his gentle manner, approached the fellow, "Like I said, we don't have a position for you, but thank you," said the coach.

"Yes, sir, I want to help with the team," the student replied. "Okay, Coach, see you tomorrow."

Totally undeterred by what the coach said, he showed up as a volunteer every day like clockwork and helped the team. He was quiet, diligent, and such a nice guy that the players soon accepted him as an integral part of the team. They even gave him a special nickname. In fact, the entire coaching staff and many fans developed a love for him as the rallying force behind the team. Season after season, he was a positive icon and inspired everyone with his spirit and tenacity. Thank goodness, he never took to heart the phrase, "Sorry, we don't have a position for you." The team did have a special job for him, but no one realized his positive impact in the beginning.

Chapter 16

WHAT MISTAKES?

1. BIG OOPS

In Zimbabwe in 2004, an unidentified bus driver was transporting 20 mental patients from the capital city of Harare to Bulawayo Mental Hospital. Along the way, he decided to stop at an illegal roadside liquor place for a few drinks. Upon his return to the bus, he was shocked to discover that all of the patients had gotten off his bus. Escaped.

Desperate for a solution, the driver thought of a quick solution. He yelled, "Free Rides, free rides" Several people climbed aboard; and then more and more, hearing the call. He had a full busload.

He promptly delivered all the sane citizens to the mental facility. He informed the hospital staff they were easily excitable. It took the medical personnel three days to uncover the foul play. During that time, the real mental patients were still at large. And, so was the driver after making his delivery.

(from "South African" newspaper)

(You caught me; I have no personal connection with this story, at all. It was such a great, zany story I had to share it.)

2. MISTAKEN IDENTITY

Many years ago, I had my house for sale. The realty company sign was out front, and I was not allowed to show the house myself. Late one afternoon, my son answered the door and let a couple come in.

He raced back to my bedroom, "Mama, there is a couple who wants to talk to you."

"Okay."

When I walked into my den, the couple was seated. So, I began my usual spiel.

I said, "If you will listen to my religious beliefs for a few minutes, then I will listen to yours." (After many people had come to my door passing out their tracts, and sharing their religion, I had prepared this response.) I said that I believed in Jesus Christ and in His Word, the Holy Bible. My faith meant a lot to me, and I was diligent in taking my children to church as well. On and on.

The couple sat very patiently until I finished my talk.

"Now, do you want to share anything with me?" I asked.

The young man spoke, "Oh, no, we just wanted to see your house."

Open mouth, insert foot.

3. ALCATRAZ

In 2005, my husband, sister-in-law, and I went to San Francisco for a cousin's wedding. My first shock was that the Golden Gate Bridge was not golden, but red. Someone had mentioned that California was the land of fruits and nuts, but I really thought they would at least know their colors.

My next surprise was how frigid the temperature was for the Fourth of July out on San Francisco Bay. My daughter had gone with her friend and family when she was in high school; she said we would need sweatshirts. She was right. Microfleece jackets were selling like hotcakes by vendors on the wharf, and all of the tourists (like us) were buying them.

After buying our tickets, we boarded the boat packed with 200 people heading out to Alcatraz Island. The waters swept down from Alaska, which caused the frigid temperatures, and cold blasts of air. The word "Alcatraz" itself denoted to most people the worst and most dreaded prison in the United States. But many famous people were imprisoned there, so it became an intriguing tourist site. Of course, the minute we boarded, Ben and Cilla were starving to death and headed straight to the snack bar. Meanwhile, everyone else scrambled to find seats. We had to split up, and I finally found a space by an older man, you know, the grandfatherly type. He seemed a little nervous. Naturally, I struck up a conversation.

"Sir, have you ever been to Alcatraz?"

"Well, uh, yes. I was IN for four years," he whispered.

I was totally stunned, and my lips were frozen shut. Finally, I squeezed out a soft, little "Oh." (I thought, *That's just great. With hundreds of people on board, I chose a seat by a former inmate.*) A million thoughts raced through my mind. Was he a killer, rapist or axe murderer? I knew he was not in Alcatraz for a speeding ticket. It had to be something serious. My heart was pounding so fast, and I knew he could sense what I was thinking. For the life of me, I could not think of one thing to say.

After an eternity of time had passed (five minutes), he said, "I wrote a book, and I am going over as the author of the day."

The color slowly returned to my face, as I stammered, "Uh...uh... good, good...uh. We will find you and buy one of your books."

We did, and from his writings discovered he had been a bank robber. I was relieved. Of course, my husband's biggest surprise was my being short on words. He remarked to others later, "Her being at a loss for words had never happened to my wife before that time. And, I don't think it has happened since."

4. MORE FLYING CREATURES

(Are you kidding me?)

At the beach, several college friends (now adults) were down in Panama City Beach staying at an exclusive condo. They were guests of the wife of Billy Payne, the phenomenal organizer of the 1996 Olympics in Atlanta. They were sitting at a table having drinks next to the open sliding glass door.

Suddenly, something swooped past their heads, but they could not see exactly what it was. Immediately, if not sooner, they started screaming and running around trying to find the "it," and not trying at the same time. They all thought it was a bat. Two of the girls sat clinging to each other and cowering in the corner. (We human beings are not crazy about bats.)

Our friend Barbara decided to go down to the office for help.

"Sir, we think there is a bat in the condo," she explained.

"Okay, we will see. Actually, we have had other calls about bats."

"Oh. What should we do?"

"I will call the pest control guy who usually comes, but it costs $200."

Barbara thought a minute, and said, "I will be right back." She headed back up to explain about the cost and discuss what they wanted to do.

Meanwhile, the terrified girls believed the bat was in a corner of the room. They watched it intently as Barbara walked back in. She looked toward the corner, and immediately headed in that direction as they screamed, "No, no, that is the bat! The bat!"

She nonchalantly walked over and picked up a crumpled Publix plastic bag as they continued their screaming. This presented a further quandary. If that wasn't the bat, then where was it? Could it be in one of the bedrooms? Barbara called the manager to tell him they had agreed to pay the $200 to the pest control dude.

An hour later, Mr. Pest Control arrived with his rat terrier. Was his rat terrier the trained bat exterminator? The dog immediately went into the rooms and jumped on the beds. They thought he might make a mess, but he jumped down. Man and dog...what a team! They snooped and sniffed and poked around. And they sniffed and poked around more. (Mainly, the terrier did all the sniffing.) Then out they came to the living room.

"Well, ladies, we cannot locate any creatures."

"Guess we still have to pay the fee," they lamented.

"Yep, that's how it works; it's a service call."

The terrier sat up begging for a doggie treat. After the guy and his ferocious animal departed, they called the office, "Well, the pest control guy came."

"Any luck?"

"No." Barbara asked the manager, "Is he usually good at this job?"

"No, not really; he has never found a bat," replied the manager.

5. IT S A LEMON

A couple had come to spend the weekend with us. At the supper table, we were discussing certain sayings that we had always heard. She said, "When you get a lemon, get rid of it."

"You are talking about a car, right? I asked.

"Well, yes and no. When you get a lemon, whether it's a car OR a husband, get rid of it as soon as possible."

(from Nancy Holshouser)

6. THE SOW ON THE LOOSE

A fellow was having trouble rounding up his huge sow, so he called his friend John to help him.

"Look here, John, I am having a problem getting my big sow back into the pen."

"Well, I've got an American bulldog that I believe will solve the problem," John replied. So, John took his bulldog to the man's farm and let him go. Sure enough, within a few minutes the sow was heading back into the pen with the bulldog in hot pursuit. The bulldog was nipping at the sow's feet, but did not stop there. The next thing they knew the bulldog had killed the sow right before their eyes. Both men were completely shocked and speechless.

Finally, John lamented, "Well, I did not know that he was gonna do that."

(from John Callaway, May 2011)

7. DIE HARD

Shouts were heard coming from a room at a nursing home in McRae, GA.

"Go on, get outta here! Go! Go!"

Several attendants dashed toward the room to help the lady in distress. They feared a male patient was bothering her. When they entered her room, they looked around, but did not see anyone.

"Are you all right, Mrs. Kline?" one asked. But she did not even look at them.

"Go on, get outta here," she yelled. Then, they realized she was watching an Atlanta Braves game. A batter had hit a long, fly ball. She was urging the ball to go over the fence.

(from my friend's mother)

Chapter 17
CRIME DIGEST

1. INEBRIATED MAN

A group of hunters had been in the field all day and were worn out. They had stayed out until almost dark and were anxious to return to camp. All were ready to kick back, talk about their adventures, and partake of some adult drinks. One was stoking the campfire, another was checking out the meat to be grilled, and the third realized they were running low on beer.

Several jumped in a truck and headed into a small town. They pulled up to a convenience store to get the beer and some gas. When the driver opened his truck door, he fell out onto the pavement. Apparently, he had been drinking excessively. Someone inside the store called the law on him.

When the police arrived, they instructed him to get back into his vehicle and follow them back to the station. Were the police crazy? Seriously, did they really ask the drunk man to drive? The answers are yes and yes. You see, requirements and compliance of laws are different in certain places, especially small towns.

2. SMALL FRY

Four bags of French fries were reported stolen Sunday from a cooler at a restaurant in the 2600 block of Irwinton Road. Gosh, it must have been a slow news week for fries to make the paper[5].

3. IT S A STEAL

A woman in the 200 block of West Bryant Street told police Monday her 17-year-old nephew stole $1,000 in cash from a pink sock she kept in her clothes hamper[6]. The real question is, if she washed the cash in the sock, was it considered money laundering?

4. HUNGRY THIEVES

A man in the 100 block of Wilson Drive discovered his residence had been burglarized Saturday afternoon. A hole had been chopped in the front door with a hatchet. Six Reeses candy bars and 10 cans of Coke were taken[7].

5. MORE HUNGRY THIEVES

A 48-year-old lady, of Madison reported several items missing from her home. Self-reported was a Philips Flat Screen TV, a pair of Air Nike tennis shoes, 30-35 DVDs, and a piece of chicken from the refrigerator. The total loss was estimated to be $850.00[8]. A large reward is offered for the missing items, but especially for that yummy piece of chicken; her husband probably ate it for a midnight snack. He is yet to admit his part of the robbery, but his dog was seen gnawing on a bone the next day.

6. SLIGHTLY HUNGRY

A woman in the 1100 block of Oconee Street said someone stole a gold bracelet Tuesday night and took two bites of some sandwich meat in her refrigerator[9].

7. CRIME CLEAN-UP

A 16-year-old girl and a 25-year-old man in the 100 block of Coombs Avenue got in a fight Sunday with a broom. The girl was hit by the broom after she tried to hit the man with it, and he blocked her attack. The man later left with a friend[10].

(The broom remained to answer questions from the authorities.)

8. NEED A WATCHDOG

A man in the 1600 block of Vinson Highway said two men kicked in his back door Tuesday night and took three watches. The crime happened while the man and his wife were in bed sleeping.

However, the man woke up "in time" to see the two men in his house. The suspects were brandishing a mop and a broom[11].

9. GOT THE DIRT ON THIS ONE

A lady we knew had really been down on her luck. We tried to help her as much as she allowed. Then, one day she said, "I have just reported a theft to the police department."

"What happened?" I asked.

"You know I had some things in the back of my truck."

"Yeah, I had noticed things occasionally."

"Someone stole my rope and a pile of dirt," she growled in an accusatory tone.

"Oh, huh, I am sorry it happened. But I am not sure if the police can identify your dirt."

She scowled at me as if she thought I took her treasures. This was added to the "Cold Case Files" recently.

Chapter 18

THINGS PEOPLE DO NOT SAY

1. TEN THINGS NORTHERNERS WILL NEVER SAY

- How's your mama and 'em?
- Let's go mud-bogging.
- I want a Loretta Lynn CD for Christmas.
- I just love grits!
- Please pass the "pot liquor."
- Ya'll come see us.
- The humidity here is very refreshing.
- Southerners have the cutest accent.
- Wish my nickname was Bubba.
- Where can I get some deer jerky?

2. TEN THINGS A SOUTHERN BOY WILL NOT SAY

- When I retire, I am moving north.
- Duct tape won't fix that.
- We don't keep firearms in this house.
- We quit hunting because it took time away from work.
- I stopped watching football because it is violent.

- Too many deer heads detract from the décor.
- The tires on that truck are too big.
- We're vegetarians here at this camp.
- I will have some fruit instead of biscuits and gravy.
- We never drink beer here.

3. A-HUNTING WE WILL GO

- Can you imagine hunters asking these questions?
- Do I get a private room with a shower?
- Can I bring Mother?
- Will it be cold?
- Is there a mall close by?
- Can I re-decorate the cabin? Is anyone allergic to smoke?
- Is beer allowed?
- Is this camouflage suit still in style?
- Did someone bring low calorie snacks?
- Do you ever see bugs, spiders, or snakes?

Chapter 19
BIRDS AND BEES

1. IN THE NEWS

Last week, I saw an interesting story about a couple being closely watched by the students at (Martha) Berry College in Rome, GA. They watched them continuously, and were extremely interested in their habits. Several students had high-powered lens on their binoculars, so they could observe minute details.

The couple, Henry and Martha, did not seem to be upset about the invasion of their privacy. Henry always did the shopping, and Martha never left the safety of their "nest." He brought home food and necessary home improvement items, such as "twigs," but not from Lowes. You see, this special couple was a pair of Bald Eagles, who built their nest on the campus. Many people had never seen this species, or the six-foot-deep, and eight foot wide nest they usually build.

The watchers noticed that whenever Henry brought a twig, or straw, Martha was never satisfied with his decorating. She always moved the twig to another place or position. Just like a **female**!

By the way, Bald Eagles mate for life, and this couple was named after Martha Berry and Henry Ford[12].

2. BEE SAFE

There will be a Henry County Beekeeper's Short Course on Saturday in McDonough. Topics covered will be:

Meeting the Bee Colony ("Hello. How are you? Nice to meet you.")

Hive Manipulation ("Look, lady, you attempt to move our hive one more time, and you will be stung…Severely!")

Extracting your Honey[13] ("Doctor, I told my husband [honey] not to get near the hives. Does he listen?)

Other Issues and Questions Facing the Beekeeper:

"What is the best way to calm my bees? Do they like certain stories?"

"How do I remind the bees that I am their friend?"

"I can't get my teenagers to do right, so how will I keep bees in line?"

3. GOD FEEDS BIRDS

God feeds the birds, but He does not throw it in their nests.

- German quotation

Chapter 20
JUST MY LUCK

1. DOG GONE IT

We had gone to visit Ben's cousins in Augusta. Anna was driving us around seeing places and running errands. We decided to pick up dinner and take it home. She called her husband.

"Hey Walt, we are getting take-out at Fish Landing. What do you want us to order for you?"

"I don't know. You can call me back."

We kept calling him to see if he had chosen something off the menu he had at home. I was getting exasperated with him, and finally asked, "I don't mean to be rude, but why can't he just make up his mind?"

Finally, his wife admitted, "Well, he can't make a decision because our dog Mopsy has eaten most of the menu, especially the entrée section."

Mopsy had heard her owners say, "Let's just eat off the menu."

2. CHANCES ARE

If your washing machine breaks down on Thursday, don't bother checking the warranty contract. It ended exactly three days ago. Believe me, our machines love to outsmart us, plus they think we are really "DUM."

If you finally find some jeans, that fit your body shape "to a T," the clothing company finds out and immediately discontinues your size and that item.

If you dial your friend on your television remote control, no matter how many times you try, no one ever will answer.

If you spill half of your coffee on your desk at work, it will become like the "Mighty Mississippi" River, soaking your work project due today, filling up your brand new expensive pocketbook, and streaking the white part of your outfit.

If your child (or grandchild) gets sick, it will be at one o'clock in the morning of the day you are leaving for your annual beach vacation.

If you buy a brand-new computer on special this Saturday with a coupon, next Saturday the store will have a huge, mark down sale. The same identical computer (or an upgrade) will be discounted $350 plus a $50 rebate.

If you get a fabulous internet deal on a quiet, hotel room with an ocean view and balcony, get ready to be surprised. Your fabulous view will also include a row of dumpsters or a cemetery, or both.

If you oversleep and tell your boss, you had a flat tire, two days later you WILL have a flat tire. Then, your excuse will be you overslept.

If your friend buys a "smart" phone, and you still have your "dumb" phone, by the time you purchase a "smart" phone, your friend has a "smarter" one. Then, things balance out when his "smarty pants" phone falls into the lake, and he loses all of his information. Now, YOU have the "smarter" phone with all your data. Life is good!

3. SECRET TO SUCCESS

In the 1990s, I met Coach Terry Sellers, the basketball coach at Georgia College as well as his family. Soon I learned that his Christian philosophy gave the players much more than just basketball skills to play the game. His positive influence built up confidence and taught them life skills beyond the college years.

Of course, he desired to have winning seasons. Constantly, he studied the game to come up with new motivational techniques and produce winning attitudes. He tells the story of getting advice when he first started his coaching career at a junior college in Alabama. A retired coach, Mr. Penny, was still on staff at the college where Terry was coaching. He understood Terry's quest to be successful.

One day, Mr. Penny said, "Hey Coach Sellers, come on by my office later. I can give you the secret to winning."

Terry could not believe his luck. He would actually find out the "the great secret" without having to seek it his entire coaching career. He was filled with anticipation and eagerness to hear what a veteran coach would impart. He excitedly walked in, and sat down in Coach Penny's office. They began talking about the game of basketball.

Finally, the old fellow said, "Coach, the secret to winning basketball is to get ahead and stay ahead."

Terry's mental balloon instantly exploded! What a disappointment!

Mr. Penny was such a great man and coach, but the secret was not really the magic bullet Terry was hoping to hear. Terry tried hard to hide his reaction. Later on, Terry's father-in-law, Mr. Cooper, knew how anxious Terry was to have a winning record. Mr. Cooper offered to talk with him, and he believed he could offer Terry some great advice on winning. Terry thought, *This time I will actually find out the secret.* He was on needles and pins awaiting the answer from Mr. Cooper.

He said, "Now, Terry, the secret to winning basketball is to put the ball through the hoop more often than your opponent."

Terry wondered, *Was this a joke or did Mr. Cooper really believe this obvious answer to winning?*

Twice, Terry Sellers NEVER received "the secret." But through years of hard work, praying, and following his faith, he brought out the best in his players; he had many winning seasons. Plus, he instilled in many young men priceless secrets to a better life for them.

(from a friend, Terry)

4. FANCY

My cousin married a doctor, and they lived in Augusta for his residency. They were invited to a big, fancy party on a Saturday night. She was always dressed in the latest style, so she immediately made an appointment at the hair salon. The hair stylist was Mr. DeMarco from New York City, who was famous, and ultra-stylish, including his black patent leather shoes. He fixed her hair in the latest hairstyle and even sprinkled in glitter to fit the occasion. They enjoyed the party that night.

Our Lovejoy grandparents were having a family reunion the next day at their house in Mt. Zion. All the relatives arrived. Aunt Vivian ("Tiny") was very tiny and plain spoken. When my cousin walked into the kitchen:

"Lordie, honey, what did you do to your hair?" Tiny inquired.

"Oh, my hair stylist, Mr. DeMarco, TEASED it," she proudly stated.

"Looks more like he INSULTED it!"

(from my husband's cousin)

5. PLUMBER, DOWN THE DRAIN

Years ago, I had a good plumber who always came right away to help me out. He was really a great guy but could not pass the test to get his license. He always fixed whatever was broken, and I even recommended his work to others. Meanwhile, he kept trying to pass the test.

One day, I saw him at the mall and said, "Hey, how are you?"

He looked at me sort of funny and replied, "You must know my twin brother, the plumber."

"Oh, yeah, I do; sorry I confused you with him."

"I'm used to that," he replied.

"By the way did he get his plumber's license?" I asked.

"Yes, he did."

A while later I called my faithful, "tried and trusted" plumber to come see about my stopped-up sink. He never returned my calls, and never came by. Can you believe that? I was surprised after I had been so supportive of him.

That just goes to show you: If a plumber gets his license, he may also get too "high falutin" for you.

And to make a long story longer…six months later, I saw that he had opened his own shop. As I was driving past it, I wanted to shake my fist at the guy and yell out my car window, "Hey, don't worry about me and my stopped-up sink!"

Luckily, the more sensible side of my brain decided maybe that was not what normal people do. (That counts me out.) Incidentally, I had gotten it fixed by another plumber.

Chapter 21

CAN YOU BELIEVE THESE?

1. FASHION FOR FEMALES

Everywhere women look, we are bombarded by being in fashion, which is a code word for "MustbeThin." Remember, the teen model, "Twiggy" in the 1960s? She was the only living person who could actually wear Barbie clothes.

Friends said, "She was so skinny, she had one stripe on her pajamas." Bless her heart. She even had to wear skiis to keep from sliding down the shower drain.

My granny said, "Looking like that just ain't nat'ural-like; if God had wanted us looking like a spaghetti noodle, why did He discover Twinkies?" Granny was quite the philosopher.

No one else during that time ever looked like Twiggy. We all hated Twiggy and her skinny self.

Mama said, "Don't say you 'hate' someone."

Okay, we disliked her intensely. And, we threw darts at her picture we had torn out of *Seventeen* magazine.

Do you remember Scarlett O'Hara from *Gone with the Wind?* Her waist (or corset measurement) was 17 inches. Now, you know that book was definitely fiction. She was so tiny, she wore a cat collar for a belt.

The cat kept following her around to get it back. Then, along came girdles that put "a real squeeze" on us, and now, we have "Spanx" to make our bodies "go where they have never gone before."

Our latest fashion magazines boast about the "So Slimming Pants" always with the "Hidden Fit Technology" that "makes you feel a size smaller." The Hidden Fit part takes effect when you wear a large Moo Moo over them. Of course, your legs will appear a size smaller. I'm glad no one told Twiggy about the "So Slimming Pants"...she would have disappeared and truly been "gone with the wind."

2. TALLER LADIES SECTION

Did I mention the models in these magazines are seven feet, 10 inches tall? Their legs measure six feet of that. Naturally, they do look fabulous in maxi-length skirts, mini-skirts, jeans, anything. They would even be knock-outs in "Pilgrim Wear." Heck, they can make a fashion statement in a burlap sack! We try our best not to **hate** these "towering over us" models. Don't mention I said that to Mama.

3. ONE MORE TWEET

(Thank you, Jesus, we cannot take any more.)

In 2004, my husband and I got married on the island of St. John in the Virgin Islands. Our ceremony was held on an idyll beach and performed by an angelic minister who strolled down with her parasol.

When we returned home, Ben loaded up all my worldly possessions and moved them to his house out in the country. Part of my world included my large rocks; he was not aware that he married the rocks too. Plus, my extensive seashell collection...I could not leave home without it. I had always dreamed of country life, so I finally would be able to experience it. Of course, we had the matching set of nature to go with it...armadillos, deer, snakes, coyotes, ducks, turtles, and birds. Some, more likable, and some less. The armadillos won the prize for the most disgusting and biggest nuisance.

During the first few weeks of marriage, I was woken up by the most robust tapping on the small window at the top of our bedroom door. A bird pecked so violently on the glass, I was afraid it might break. (The glass, as well as its beak.) What was it with these crazed birds? This bizarre tapping occurred every morning, but only came when my husband was not present in the room. The weird tap, tap, tapping reminded me of the rap, rap, rapping of the raven from Edgar Allen Poe's tale.

Eventually, I had a heart to heart talk with the bird. I shook my finger at that crazy bird and said, "Nevermore."

4. HOODWINKED BY A HOOD?

A young state patrolman had pulled onto a small dirt road and parked his patrol car beside a thick growth of bushes and trees. He watched as the traffic went by on the main road and monitored their speed. Sure enough, within a few minutes, a red sports car came flying past him with the music blaring and the mufflers rumbling. He clocked its speed at least 20 miles per hour over the limit. His heart beat a little faster as he fumbled to switch on the engine; it was his first week working solo.

He turned on the blue flashing lights and gunned it in pursuit of the culprit. Finally, the car slowed down and pulled over. He got out, took a deep breath, grabbed his ticket book, walked up to the car, and looked into the window. He was surprised to see an older lady driving such a souped-up vehicle.

"Ma'am, did you realize you were speeding?"

"Oh… yes, sir, Officer, of course I knew."

"You did?" asked the shy officer, "Can you, perhaps, explain why?"

"Sure, I can. You see I'm in such a hurry to get home to get these tight pantyhose off," explained the lady, who was a friend of ours. "You understand, don't you?"

"Oh…hmm…well…okay…um," stammered the embarrassed officer.

"Got to go, officer."

"Well, um…keep moving, then," he mumbled as she tore off with her wheels spinning in the grass.

5. WHAT'S IN A NAME?

I met a lady at our church with the last name of Goode. I said, "You have a wonderful name."

She replied, "So do you," when she saw Lovejoy on my name tag. "It seems like something funny always happens," she continued.

"Quick story. I teach first grade. One year on the first day of school, I had a boy named Will in my class. When he was picked up by his mother. Naturally, she asked, 'How did school go?'

"'Fine.'

"'What is your teacher's name?'

"He replied, 'I think it is Miss Nice.'"

The next time I see her, I have a "name" story for her. My uncle's name was Harry Looney. You can imagine the ribbing he got his whole life. He loved to joke about it and always had funny stories to tell. As a furniture salesman, he and his wife Gertrude attended conventions all over the United States. So, he met a lot of people. One day a man reached out to shake his hand, and said, "My name is Silly."

"Looney here. Great to meet you," my uncle answered.

Could my craziness be hereditary?

6. WILL THIS PAIR EVER PAR?

An elderly man was playing on a golf course by himself one morning. He noticed there was a lady golfer playing behind him. He stopped her and said, "Little lady, I have a problem. My eyesight is so bad that I can't follow the ball. How is your eyesight?"

"Well, my eyesight is great, but my memory is slipping," she responded.

"In that case, when I hit the ball, would you watch it and tell me where it lands?"

"Sure, I will be glad to," she said.

So, the ole fellow hit the ball down the fairway. He turned to her and asked, "How was that drive?"

"Perfect," she said.

"Where did it go?"

"I forgot." (from our beloved friend, "Mac" McSwain, Columbia, SC)

7. NICE COMBINATIONS

Unique restaurants in St. John, Virgin Islands: "Chilly Willy" was the breakfast place, and "Ten Tables" was for dinner. They used the exact same location for the two restaurants. After breakfast, they re-arranged the space, and only set up 10 tables for dinner. What a clever idea to economize! We enjoyed eating at both.

Hair salon and service station in Brunswick, GA. Get your hair shampooed and your oil changed. (No, you probably don't need your oil changed.) My daughter got her hair fixed while her girlfriend got an oil change for her car.

Video and Tan in Ducktown, TN. Get a tan while your friend picks out a great chick flick.

Hair Salon and Headstone Store. (I promise this is true) Get your hair fixed while your husband goes across the aisle and picks out your tombstone. Or after you have your hair fixed, pick out your own tombstone...a much more expensive one. I would not have believed this unless I had gone with friends to see it. It was at a unique, permanent sheltered flea market in Pendergrast, GA.

A girl named Raunchie. When you look at this name, it is fine, but when you say it out loud, it sounds terrible. She was one of my customers at the bank.

Chapter 22
MY ESSAYS AND RAMBLINGS

1. THE INHERITANCE

Years ago, I inherited my parents' antique pump organ that we all had enjoyed playing. When our own kids came along, they pulled the knobs in and out, pumped the pedal, and played tunes on it, more or less, too. By the time I received the pump organ, it was broken. My family moved the heavy piece to a repairman who lived in the tiny hamlet of Sunnyside, Georgia. His shop was right behind his house.

Three years passed, and not a word from him. He had the same philosophy we had heard our friend say, "You just can't rush into these things." When I finally talked to "Mister-Not-So-Sunnyside," he said, "I cannot repair it because these parts are not available anymore."

"Well, we will come to your shop to pick it up." So, we did.

When we arrived, he informed me, "Someone else has been working on this pump organ."

"No sir, that is not true. Please excuse my rudeness, but the only repairman was you." I had been to his shop before.

"Hmm...I see."

I called an antique/junk dealer and told him my woeful tale of the ailing piece.

"Sir, can you sell it in your antique store?"

"I can try, but no promises."

"Do you have any people who can move it?"

"We have some moving guys who can do that," he replied. He implied he had no connection with them.

"What is the cost from Sunnyside to McDonough?"

"Hmm, $100 that you pay to a lady here" (whom he seemed to hardly know.).

"I want to set up the day and time."

So, the lady took the phone and set up the arrangements.

On the assigned day, I arrived to meet the moving guys. Surprise! Surprise! One of the movers was the exact same guy on the phone, "Go over to that lady, and pay your money." I looked around the store, walked up and down, but no lady. Their philosophy seemed to be, "Why make it easy on your customer when it is funnier to watch him wander around the store?"

"Where is the lady?" I finally asked.

"She is behind that desk."

I headed toward the tall desk, and still saw no one. Then, up she popped, like a jack-in-the-box.

"Do you have a check for the movers?"

"Yes."

"You can make it out to me. I am his wife," as she pointed to her swindler husband I had spoken to. *This is definitely a crazy racket they have here. No one seems connected until you arrive; then, it is a husband and wife tag team,* I thought to myself. Finally, the movers brought the pump organ back to the bilker/chiseler store.

"Can you price it for $400?" I asked.

"Hmm…let's put $800 on it," Mr. Swindler said.

"Okay." (Darn, does this story ever end?)

So, every couple of years I go into the cheater/antique store walk right past the rogue couple, who never recognize me, and head to the back of the store. I sit down and spend time with my inheritance piece, feeling sentimental. After a few years, they lowered the price to $400. Still, no one bought it.

However, I am confident my treasured inanimate heirloom misses me. As the years have passed, I have continued to stop by and spend time with my "family" piece. I am in a quandary...what should I do? I am giving it five more years, and if no one has bought it, I have made up my mind. I am buying it back. (Oh, yeah, I forgot; I already own it.)

2. LEFTOVERS

As the holiday season winds down, we all wonder what to do with that leftover turkey. And I am not talking about Uncle Slim...the leftover... who is still visiting you after three days. If you are Suzy Homemaker, you make a variety of dishes using turkey instead of chicken, such as turkey pot pie and various specialties which are disguised. (A lot of men say they hate casseroles.) Next, you label and freeze all of them. (The casseroles, not the men.) Then on a cold, wintry night in February or March, when the turkey enzymes have left your bodies, you invite the neighbors over for eats and treats. You start by introducing them to one of the world's most exhilarating pastimes: "The Casserole Game." (Trust me, no matter how hard you try, men know a casserole when they see it.)

Here is how the game goes: Your neighbor says, "I can name that casserole in three bites." He tastes it, tries to guess what it is, but misses.

So, your husband counters, "I can name that casserole in two bites."

And so, the eating game goes until everyone is full. Best of all, you have fed your neighbors until they are stuffed, and you have no leftover turkey. Except for Uncle Slim.

3. RECYCLING

Did I mention fruit cake? (No, I am past the subject of Uncle Slim, believe it or not.) When we were growing up, everyone loved to send fruitcakes to friends and relatives. I really do not know why. It seems very few people really liked to eat them. One family always received a fruit cake from the same neighbor each year. They despised the taste of it. When she came to the front door, their mother yelled to the son.

"Billy, Mrs. Whoody is at the door."

"Yes, ma'am," answered Billy. "Hello, thank you for the fruit cake."

"You are welcome, and I hope you will enjoy it."

"We will," he lied. Immediately, little Billy took the fruit cake, as instructed by his mother, and headed down the hallway and out the back door, and slung it into the ditch, their official dump. The wasps and flies looked forward to it all year long.

Since many fruitcakes were re-gifted and circled the world nine times, they were very hard and brick-like. If you were resourceful, you could wrap it with thick material…made a perfect doorstop. The next year, you could re-gift it.

4. WHAT SHE SAID

Most of us need help in communicating with each other. We use common words and speak the same language…Southern. What is our problem? Women talk; men pretend to listen. Do not ask your husband a question about anything you have just said. You are definitely looking for trouble.

Every once in a while, I ask my husband, "Exactly what is your mind doing when I am talking?"

He replies with, "Can you repeat that question?"

You see, he was not even listening when I asked the question. If I ask him, "What is your mind doing?" he says, "It is visiting the planets." Translation: "day dreaming." According to good sources (whom we do not know), it is proven that when women are saying words, the man only hears, "Blah, blah, blah, and blah." We now believe that men's ear flaps are anatomically made different. When we say a word, their ear flaps can only tune in to certain signals and decibels. The men cannot help it; that is how God made them.

Women display extreme reactions to this gigantic communication dilemma; they think shouting, stomping their feet, or yelling, "Never mind!" as they noisily leave the room will help. Maybe, their antics will draw sufficient attention for their husbands to realize there is a problem. Wrong! My newest strategy is to ask the same question every few hours, and possibly, I get a coherent answer within a few days or so.

Once my son said, "Mama, you keep asking him the same thing." (And my husband was in the car with us when he asked.)

"Oh, I know, but he hasn't heard me yet."

You just have to be patient. And wait for a government study costing $5 million as to why men's ears only hear "blahs" or "supper is ready."

5. MERRY OLE ENGLAND

Several years ago, my two sisters and I took a very special "sister trip" to London, England. One particular interest was visiting Highclere Castle, where the drama "Downton Abbey" was filmed. Before we left,

Marilyn, the middle sister, remarked, "I hope we are still sisters when we return...I don't want to divorce y'all." We all laughed!

She was our official trip planner and guide. She reminded us, "Don't forget to take some washcloths because the hotels in England don't have them." What is wrong with these people? I'll bet they give washcloths to everyone, but Americans. They are probably still mad about the Boston Tea Party a while back. We had heard, "You must have English adapters and chargers, if you plan to plug in anything," and most women have three or four things minimum. We carry all sorts of indispensable gadgets with plugs. (I believe strange voltage and wattage were among the reasons the Pilgrims left England for the New World.)

Our oldest and adorable sister, Dianne, said, "On a previous trip, I melted my hair using my curling iron without a special foreign adapter. I saw and smelled smoke as my hair melted, and stayed on the curling iron. Wispy, burned hair and a lack of it was not a good look on me; I needed to pull a hat down over my ears." As sweet, sympathetic sisters, we patiently listened to her tale of woe and felt within our hearts her time of misery. Then, we fell onto the floor laughing our heads off.

Someone commented, "The great thing about going to England is they speak the same language—English."

"Yeah, right," I said. "They do, but we don't! We speak Southern."

At Kensington Palace, a nice chap in a shop asked me, "Have you seen all the puppies round the tower?"

"Uh, uh...no, I haven't," I replied, being very puzzled by the question. "Are they alive?" I asked.

"Oh, no, they are not live."

I thought to myself, *I am NOT going to see all those dead puppies. He must be a real sicko.* Then, I realized what he was saying: "Poppies." They were making around 884,000 gorgeous, ceramic poppies for the 100-Year Commemoration of all the British soldiers and personnel who died in World War I. Each poppy was carefully made by hand and placed around the Tower of London. What a magnificent sight it was to see! One of my grandest memories of the whole trip!

6. WHAT KEY?

When we were in high school, it was common practice for freshman boys to be the recipients of jokes played on them. Several coaches and personnel had schemes to confuse these boys on the first day of school. For example, Coach A called in two freshmen, "Okay, I have an errand for you. Head over to see the Athletic Director, Coach B, and ask him for a certain key."

"Yes, sir."

They found Coach B, and asked him, "Do you have the key to the batters' box?"

"No, someone misplaced it; go talk to Coach C."

"Yes, sir, we will."

Coach C, the baseball coach, responded, "I believe the manager left it in the equipment room."

When they got to the room, Coach A, B and C were all there.

Coach A asked, "Well, boys, any luck?"

"No, sir."

"Okay, here is the deal...there is no such thing as a key to the batters' box."

All the coaches cracked up laughing in unison. That same day, Coach C nabbed two different freshmen, "Hey, young men, we are looking for the sky hook that belongs to the track coach. Go see if she has found it."

Coach D, the track coach, was down at the field house.

"Coach D, have you located the sky hook?" they asked.

"Not yet," she responded, "but maybe Coach E has it."

When they found Coach E, he said, "No," as he choked back a laugh. "And the only way you will ever find it is to invent one...there is no such thing."

Until this day we are still confused about something...spaghetti seeds. We were sent to the biology teacher to find them, but he did not know. Everyone seemed clueless. Just one of life's many mysteries.

7. TUMBLEWEED TALI

Some people are naturally accident prone; others attain the status. Mine has developed through the years. I have been a good example of Murphy's Law: If anything can go wrong, it will. No one knows when or how things began, but the name Calamity Jane came to mind. She was a Western sharpshooter who led a life of many opposites, with things constantly going wrong, and she was always at the center of trouble. Since her name was already taken, I took the moniker "Tumbleweed Tali."

When I was six years old, I broke two bones in my foot. In those days, they were super cautious and put a full-length leg cast on my right leg. My doctor said, "Don't worry, your cast will only stay on for 3 months."

A week later, I woke up with the mumps. Guess I was unlucky from the beginning.

As the years went by, I was run over by a go cart, almost bit my tongue off playing football, was knocked out by baseballs and softballs, and was pummeled by boards as our tree house bit the dust. Not to mention all the times I was bucked off a horse or pony. In the eighth grade, I contracted rheumatic heart fever and a murmur. I missed a lot of school, so rumors and gossip were running rampant. When I returned to school, I was shocked; my class stood up and clapped.

I asked, "What is going on?"

"We thought you were dying, and we were choosing another cheerleader to take your place."

"Oh, I didn't know I was dying."

In high school, I got on a motorcycle with my love crush and sizzled my leg on the exhaust pipe. That burn was definitive proof for my punishment of being on a motorcycle, which was strictly forbidden. As an adult, I bought a new bike to get in shape. One day, I hit a rock, flipped the bike, and my helmet (with my head inside) struck the ground. After dealing with three cracked teeth followed by two implants, I decided to trade in my bike for a tricycle.

As "Tumbleweed Tali," I have learned that trying to exercise and stay in shape is dangerous for my health. I know what you are thinking: I could have avoided many of my mishaps. That is right. I could have stayed inside…played with dolls, tea sets, and girly things…more of the time. The truth is, I tried to play with paper dolls, but making their clothes stay on with those little tabs was a nightmare. Those tabs did not work and made no sense. Too much stress for a little kid!

Besides, if I had stayed in, just think of all the fun I would have missed.

8. SERIOUS WRITERS

Writing elegant and flowing passages is extremely difficult. Even the great writers scream, throw things, and rip up pages in their quest to squeeze the exact word or phrase from their brain that fits succinctly into the niche. For some bizarre reason, we think that writers sit down, and that perfectly formed, beautiful sentences flow from their feathery plumes like the Amazon River. Untrue. Most writers face the same agonizing conundrum that we untrained writers do: they struggle with the tedious task of getting the words on paper that satisfy the meaning and the sound they seek. Sometimes, getting a specific story to sound flawless, or close to it may take years.

For instance, a writer starts a piece, edits over and over, rereads it later, but it does not express what he wants with any clarity. Frustrated, he stashes the project in a drawer and forgets about it. Then, one day while fishing through his desk drawers, he re-discovers the "forgotten pearl." As he reads his writing again, he edits with more ease, and the words begin to flow. Within a deep, secluded spot in the inner mind, the ideas and phrases have tumbled around continuously. The writer is totally unaware of the subconscious at work. The meaning of his "pearl" has begun to unravel itself toward a clearness of thought and understanding. The clarification gem yearns to break through and present itself if the writer can pen the clearest words on paper before the ideas escape and evaporate.

9. WRITING A BOOK

Have you read a book before and thought to yourself, "I could have written that book, or a better one"? Or, you are telling entertaining stories to your friends, and someone says, "You should write a book."

"Yes, I should," you respond.

But most people will never write that book. Why? The truth about writing involves tons of willpower and concentration. You make yourself sit in a chair for hours on end and churn out words on paper or a computer. Sounds easy, but it is a very difficult and lonely task. Even if you enjoy writing, there are 100 distractions to jolt you out of your seat. At home, you have daily cleaning, washing clothes, tending to your children, texting friends, and fixing meals. Life, in general, keeps you from writing. Also, if you like to socialize with friends, the hours melt away, and your computer sits idle. Spending hours on social media and television can take your precious time, and you have nothing concrete to show for it.

However, getting out in the world gives me a new outlook, and I enjoy spending the treasured time with my friends and family. That time fills me with a brightness and fulfillment, so I can return home and start writing again. Often, a change of scenery, the bright sunshine, or a relaxing walk in the woods can bring renewed thoughts. Plus, freeing your mind to think other things can bring serendipitous results. A word or an idea may pop into your head that fits succinctly into that cantankerous sentence you are battling. That revelation is called a "bolt out of the blue."

10. DEFINITE SIGNS YOU NEED TO RETIRE

Every time your boss walks by, your foot automatically springs forward to trip him.

If you have to attend one more meeting, you start speaking in unknown languages and your mind goes into a permanent trance.

The last time you smiled was 1989.

When a customer asks you a question that you have answered 8,345 times, you have an uncontrollable urge to bang your head on your desk.

If you attend one more promotion event when the youngest employee gets a huge promotion and raise, you start sticking out your tongue, and saying, "Nanny, Nanny, Boo Boo."

You have a lot of headaches from banging your head. (See # 4.)

If you hiss and claw at your clients, start filling out the retirement forms immediately.

11. OUT IN THE STICKS

We live about eight miles from Sparta, so big city people think we live way out in the country. Occasionally, we go to Atlanta to a wedding or party, and sometimes we may not know many guests. When I meet new people, I always ask them where they are from or where they live now. If this is a situation that we know we will never see them again, I can really get their attention.

"We live way out in the country…so far out that the sun sets between our house and the mail box." They laugh. "We have all kinds of wildlife—coyotes, snakes, deer, foxes, rabbits, possums, armadillos, and chipmunks."

Once, my sister-in-law was telling folks in the big city about all these creatures. One lady asked, "My dear, how do you live with all those wild beasts?"

Now, these city slickers cannot imagine dealing with these creatures, so they look at me like I have two heads. And, that's when I kick it up a notch.

"And most all of them live in the house with us when they are babies. Especially, the coyote babies…they can be quite adorable, you know," I add.

Now, they are elbowing each other. One lady asks, "What do you do about those horrid armadillos?"

My husband replies, "Well, you would be surprised how smart they are. We have actually trained them to pull little wagons out in the fields. The chipmunks pick up fallen limbs and fill up the wagons. It is quite a timesaver for us."

The people want to get away from us but cannot think how they will do it without being rude.

"Oh, yeah, we have river otters; I forgot to mention them. They are so slick and beautiful. Some of the smarter ones we teach to do back flips over the dam. A few of them we sold to the traveling circus. But then, we missed them so much that we bought them back."

The look on their faces (the people, not the otters) is priceless. For some reason—I don't know why—they act fidgety and usually start backing away.

Then one interjects, "Excuse me, I am going to get another drink." The others stumble over each other and turn quickly around to follow. Then, we bust out laughing. When country comes to town, we surely have fun. (This story was a figment of my imagination.)

Chapter 23

UNIQUE EXPERIENCES

1. VALENCIA, SPAIN, 1970

When I was 20 years old, I was selected to join the Study Aboard Program along with 34 other students from Georgia. Janice Andrews, a student from my college, Georgia Southern, was my roommate. She and I had many adventures. Immediately, we tried the Spanish cuisine in addition to the meals we ate at home. Almost every day after our culture class, Janice and I went to a bar to taste the particular wines our professor had discussed. Early on, we saw someone eating onion rings and ordered some by pointing at theirs. Little did we know it was squid legs until we tasted the slight sponginess.

The most exciting adventure was hitchhiking up and down the coast of Spain. At that time, hitching a ride was not a dangerous thing in Spain. We would never have considered it back at home. On one trip, we went to Benidorm, a beautiful beach resort, and stayed at a student hostel, which was very cheap with one bathroom for everyone. At the end of the summer, we took a train from Madrid to Paris. We barely made the train and ran, dragging our suitcases to jump on. We endured one of the coldest nights of our lives. The windows were wide open, and my thin blanket did not help much. We stayed in Paris for five nights. When we stood in front of the Eiffel Tower, I was overcome emotionally. I never imagined a small-town girl like me would ever see something so magnificent.

When we flew back into New York, I had one quarter left (in American currency), and that was exactly what the bus ride to the main terminal cost. Finally, we arrived in Atlanta. My family did not recognize me. I was wearing Spanish clothes, had changed my hairstyle and was darkly tanned. I walked right past them.

2. BEACH MINISTRY, 1971

I left the comfort of my family and friends during the summer of 1971 for a different kind of experience. I was 21 years old, and wanted to go to a place where I knew no one and see if I could survive. My parents thought I had lost my mind. I got a position with a beach ministry in Port Aransus on Mustang Island, Texas. (The name even sounded exciting). The ministry was backed by five churches, and our mission was to help runaways, drug addicts, and cult members learn about Jesus Christ. We had our work cut out for us.

"Your salary will be one dollar a day," my mother said.

My dad just shook his head.

"Yes, but it will include food, housing, and other expenses," I added.

I was relieved to meet my hosts at the airport. The husband, wife, and two sons were welcoming, and I felt good about my family for the summer. Soon, I met the two other girls with our ministry.

What an awakening the summer held for me! Many experiences were scary and very far removed from my world. So much of what I learned was very difficult to see. I met young people whose lives had been destroyed by drugs. A 14-year-old girl had been on LSD, and as we were talking, she slipped into a trance. Her brain was fried. Then, after a few minutes she woke up. I counseled with runaways, whose lives had no direction, goals, or hope. We prayed that our talks about Jesus would make a difference for them.

The worst influence was the different cults that invaded the beach each summer. I talked with cult members, who appeared to be the answer, but they preyed on the vulnerability of these young people who flocked to this place. I met a blonde-headed, nice-looking guy who spoke Bible verses with great conviction, but living with the Children of God, he was a captive. The cult took away his name and gave him a new identity; they took all his possessions and turned him against his family. Every day, he was brainwashed for hours on end with verses until he sounded almost robotic. He could not leave the cult or have any contact his parents. Later, I found out many parents had an extremely difficult time getting their children away from this cult. Once the young people got back home, they endured intense counseling to readjust to a normal life again.

We had a huge fish bake for all the homeless and runaways. We dug a large pit in the sand, and local fishermen donated fish to our worthy cause. Our ministry lacked money to do many things, but the fish bake along with the sides fed many people and was a big success.

We did have fun during our time there. On our off days, the two sons taught us how to gig flounders at midnight in a shallow bay. It was a little spooky sloshing through the water carrying a lantern in the moonlight. We were reminded of the movie, *The Creature from the Black Lagoon.* They took us crabbing and showed us how to catch a crab with a string, piece of meat, and a dipping net. We loved every minute of our adventures with them.

With God's help and my wonderful summer family, I not only survived the beach ministry in Texas, but had life-changing experiences as well. My faith and courage were greatly challenged, but I left with great memories.

3. THE DOUBLE RAINBOWS

Before we left for home, our family drove us southward along the flat endless beach which stretched for miles. They wanted us to see South Padre Island. It was misting rain. Suddenly a giant rainbow encompassed the total horizon…the highway was taking us straight into and through the prism of colors. None of us had ever seen such a spectacular sight. Then, a second rainbow displayed its magnificence over the first one. We were speechless, seeing these beautiful signs from God, and were reminded of His Promise to never flood the earth again. As we continued, the setting sun broke through and temporarily blinded us with its uncompromising brightness. We had to pull off the road until our driver could see again. What we experienced could never be a planned event, which made everything more amazing.

4. MELTING OF CULTURES, 2006

We were vacationing on St. John in the U.S. Virgin Islands. One night, we dined at one of our favorite restaurants, "The Balcony," a stone's throw to the beach. Tropical breezes flowed through this open-air restaurant as we soaked in the total atmosphere: small waves lapping at the shore, lights shining from boats moored close by, and the delicious aromas floating in the air. Caribbean music emanated from a musical combo, and we were captured by its throbbing and distinctive beat. Their vocalist's voice mesmerized the crowd. We were tapping our toes to the beat, and could not resist getting up to dance. We noticed the waitresses swaying to the rhythm. I motioned for them to join us on the tiny dance floor. They flashed their beautiful smiles and moved toward us, dancing their unique calypsos. Soon we tried to imitate their movements, and they were pleased at our efforts toward gyrations that were so natural to them. Our hips, legs, and arms were awkward at first, and we all laughed together. Nothing mattered.

A special moment occurred when our smiles spoke their language; skin color and culture no longer divided us. We embraced our togetherness. We were no longer foreigners who spoke or thought differently; we were friends of the universe. No words were necessary as we sensed the warmth of their hospitality. We felt a kinship, a oneness. Through the sharing of their rich music and motions, we melted into their culture. For those magical, spontaneous moments, our minds and souls connected on a level I have never experienced. I will never forget the beauty and simplicity of that time.

5. WHAT BLACK DOTS? 2016

One afternoon I was driving home after having lunch with two friends. As I was crossing the last bridge before reaching home, I saw something bizarre. In the distance, I saw tiny black dots moving through the air on the opposite side of the Oconee River. They appeared to be traveling together...whatever they were. I turned my car off the main road onto a smaller road and stopped. Focusing on this phenomenon, I could not keep driving safely to solve the mystery of the moving dots; total concentration was indispensable. As the dots got closer and bigger, I got nervous; they seemed to be heading straight toward me. Although I was within the confines of my car, anxiety ruled my mind. Within minutes, they struck my car. I realized it was hundreds of bees. Many died on impact with my windshield. I still did not know why they came toward me. Then, I learned that bees fly directly to their nearest source of nutrition. I was an obstacle in their bee line, and they did not waver from their route. My advice: Bee careful!

6. THE STRANGEST ENCOUNTER, 2018

My husband and I were paddling our little john boat up Shoulderbone Creek. Quietly sliding through the water, we guided our boat along the grass-covered shore. On the edge of the bank, I noticed a strange animal standing upright. A river otter. We were surprised because we had never considered the fact that otters had feet to support their weight. We had watched otters as their sleek bodies slid along the surface of the water. Searching for fish, they dove down causing huge, circular ripples that moved across the creek. We sighted the precious babies by following a line of tiny bubbles below the surface of the water. Being so close to the bank, we had a clear view of them.

But this encounter was unique; the otter still as a statue stared at us for several moments, not in fear, but with a look of curiosity. We did not move a muscle and held our breaths. I looked the otter straight in the eye as we gazed at this amazing creature, out of its normal habitat. We knew the slightest move or change would scare it away. We were mesmerized with its calmness. It was a spectacular meeting of a human and wild animal, where stillness displaced any feelings of fear. We observed and drank in that amazing moment, knowing our time was fleeting. We did not want this serendipitous meeting to end. What were the chances of seeing an otter close up again? In all of our years being attuned to nature and our surroundings, neither of us had experienced a perfect moment like this. Gently, the otter moved away and swam into the cool waters and was gone.

Bibliography

Jeff Nesmith, "100th Birthday Party is Ho-Hum for Her," *Atlanta Journal-Constitution*, January 31, 2008.

Baker, Pearl, *A Handbook History of McDuffie County*, (1870-1970) (Atlanta: Progress-New Publishing Company, 1971), 44-45.

Harrington, Marlene, *Tales from a Farr* (Milledgeville: Studio Design Printing, 1998), p.55.

Ibid., p.56.

"Crime Digest," *The Union Recorder*, June 23, 1998, 8.

"Milledgeville Police Department," *The Union Recorder*, July 9, 1998, 12.

"Crime Digest," *The Union Recorder*, July 27, 1998, 9.

"Crime Digest," *Lake Oconee News*, January 21, 1999, 11.

"Crime Digest," *The Union Recorder*, February 4, 1999, 8.

Ibid., April 10, 2000, 9.

Ibid., May 22, 2000, 8.

"Berry College Watches Martha and Henry," *CNN, Headline News*, January 13, 2012.

"Workshop on Bees," *Henry County Times*, January 10, 2013, 11.

CPSIA information can be obtained
at www.ICGtesting.com
Printed in the USA
LVHW051719120121
676311LV00035B/297